Free Trade and Markets in Healthcare
Lessons from Asian Countries

Free Trade and Markets in Healthcare

Lessons from Asian Countries

Editors

Philip Stevens

Debashis Chakraborty

SYNERGY BOOKS INDIA

(A imprint of Bookwell Publications)

New Delhi

Free Trade and Markets in Healthcare
Lessons from Asian Countries

First Edition 2013

ISBN: 978-93-82059-15-8

Synergy Books India
(A imprint of M/s Bookwell Publications)
24/4800 Ansari Road, Darya Ganj
New Delhi-110002
Phone: 011-23268786, 23257264
Fax: 011-23281315
E-Mail: synergybooksindia@gmail.com
bookwell@vsnl.net

Printed in India at Mudrak, 30-A, Patparganj, Delhi-110091.

CONTENTS

Section 2
The Role of the Private Sector in Health
Asian experiences

Author Biographies

Prof. Yu Hui

Prof. Hui is a research fellow in the Chinese Academy of Social Sciences and Director of China Research Center for Public Policy. Yu is a specialist on the economics of regulation and industrial organizations, and was involved in the process of legal drafting on anti-monopoly law, telecommunications law and the regulations of electricity supervision. His recent research focuses on China's overseas investment, healthcare and educational system reform.

Prof. Xingyuan Feng

Prof. Xingyuan Feng is Associate Professor at the Rural Development Institute (RDI) of the Chinese Academy of Social Sciences, Vice-Director of the Unirule Institute of Economics and Research, Associate East-West Centre for Business Studies and Cultural Science, Frankfurt School of Finance and Management.

He is also a co-founder and Vice President of the Cathay Institute for Public Affairs, a think tank in Beijing, and editor-in-chief of a new book series in China, Theory of Order and Economics.

Dr. Amir Ullah Khan

Amir Ullah Khan is an economist working on trade policy issues. Amir studied at the Institute of Rural Management at Anand and obtained his PhD from the Jamia Millia Central University in New Delhi. He is Senior Fellow at the India Development Foundation and also teaches Economic Policy at the Centre for Executive Education at the Indian School of Business in Hyderabad

Dr. Debashis Chakraborty

Dr. Chakraborty is Assistant Professor of Economics at the Indian Institute of Foreign Trade, a position he has held since January 2006. Previously, he was Research Associate at Rajiv Gandhi Institute for Contemporary Studies, New Delhi.

He is an expert on international trade and the WTO, and has written on a number of Indian economic and human development issues.

Bienvenido "Nonoy" Oplas

Mr. Oplas heads the Minimal Government Thinkers, a free market think tank in Manila, He writes a weekly column in www.interaksyon.com, the news portal of TV5 and in www.thelobbyist.biz, an online magazine. He published his first book, "Health Choices and Responsibilities" in 2011. He is also a member of the DOH Advisory Council on Healthcare, the Coalition for Health Advocacy and Transparency (CHAT), and the Philippine Economic Society (PES). He graduated from the University of the Philippines School of Economics (UPSE).

Philip Stevens

Mr. Stevens founded the Emerging Markets Health Network in 2012. Previously, he was research director at International Policy Network, a UK-based think tank, research associate at the Adam Smith Institute, as well as holding a number of roles in business and consultancy.

Fredrik Erixon

Fredrik Erixon is a Swedish Economist and Writer. He is the Director of the European Centre for International Political Economy (ECIPE), a world-economy think tank based in Brussels he co-founded in 2006.

Prior to starting ECIPE, Erixon was an Adviser to the British government and the Chief Economist of Timbro, a Swedish think tank. He started his career as an economist in the Prime Ministers Office in Sweden and has later worked as an economist at the World Bank and for JP Morgan as an emerging market analyst.

Ali Salman

Ali Salman is a development consultant, policy entrepreneur and economic analyst based in Islamabad, Pakistan, where he heads Policy Research Institute of Market Economy. Ali is author of several studies and monographs including the path-breaking *Liberate to Learn: Review of Education Vouchers Scheme in Lahore* by Alternate Solutions Institute, a critique of price controls *Price Controls: Implications for Liberty and Welfare*, and *Discord between Economic Freedom and Social Justice in Islam.*

Mehreen Zahid Malik

Mehreen Zahid Malik has a Bachelor in Economics and Mathematics from the Lahore University of Management Sciences, Lahore, and she worked on her chapter while a Research Associate at Alternate Solutions Institute in Pakistan. Mehreen is currently working as an Assistant Manager Compliance, with the Assessment and Strengthening Program (ASP), a joint project of USAID and the Lahore University of Management Sciences (LUMS).

INTRODUCTION
TRADE, HEALTH AND THE MARKET: CHALLENGES FOR ASIA

Debashis Chakraborty and Philip Stevens

The Background

The proposition that markets are the most efficient way to allocate scarce resources, drive innovation and create economic growth is relatively uncontroversial. Liberalising market reforms in general lead to greater competition, and the resulting domestic efficiency leads to export opportunities and sustainable economic growth, as has been amply demonstrated by myriad countries from the United Kingdom to China. It is therefore not surprising that countries enjoying greater economic freedom also enjoy higher levels of per capita GDP (in terms of Purchasing Power Parity) (Miller et al, 2012).

More liberalized domestic and global markets have been instrumental in driving up living standards in almost all countries over the last fifty years, with the exception of countries that have chosen to isolate themselves, such as North Korea. Nevertheless, the perceived imperfections of markets have ensured that government has continued to play a dominant role in healthcare provision, not just as a regulator and facilitator, but also as a provider (Wu and Ramesh, 2009). This phenomenon is particularly evident in lower and middle-income countries. While government dominance and nationalisation of sectors such as manufacturing, transport, telecommunication, food production and retail has resulted in spectacular and well-documented failures, the adverse welfare implications of limiting the role of the market in healthcare are less accepted. Nevertheless, some countries have begun to experiment with more liberal approaches to healthcare, both in terms of global trade and domestic provision.

Figure 1: Relationship between Economic Freedom and Growth

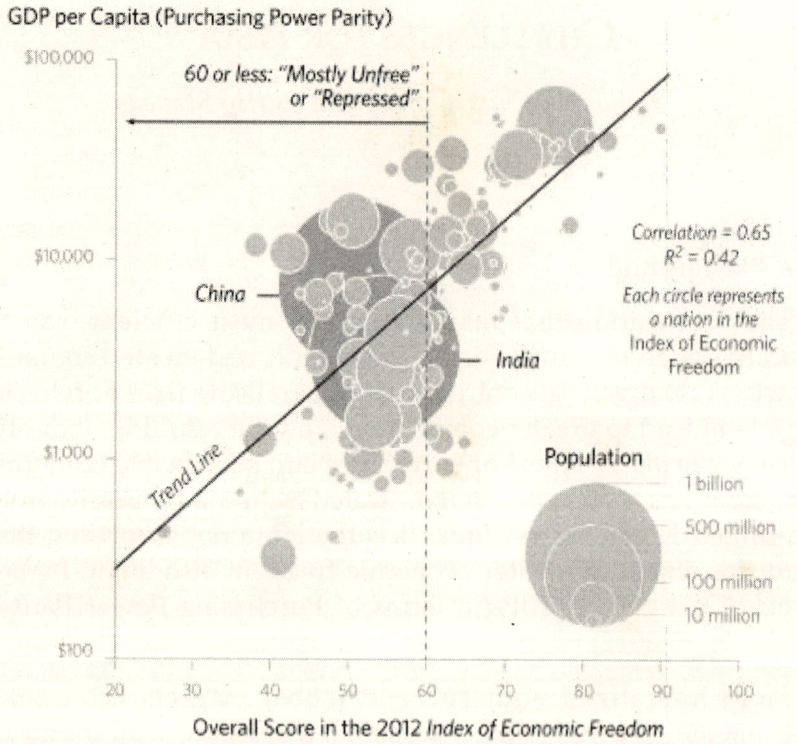

Source: Quoted from Miller et al (2012)

The world today faces several health-related challenges. High income countries are facing ageing populations, and as a result, an increasing burden of chronic such as heart disease, cancer, pulmonary conditions etc. Most lower and middle-income countries are also facing similar rises in the burden of these non-communicable diseases, while also continuing to struggle to meet Millennium Development Goals (MDGs), such as reducing child mortality rates, improving maternal health and combating HIV/AIDS, malaria, TB and other similar diseases. Although several countries have performed commendably on the MDG front, there is still some distance to travel to end current high-rates of preventable disease and death (UNCTAD, 2011).

For lower and middle-income countries, the MDGs are just one component of a bigger picture. To entrench health security in a country, it is imperative to ensure expansion of health infrastructure, establish a policy framework to allow the development of affordable and simpler health insurance schemes etc. among other things. On both counts, the private sector has a major role to play in fulfilling the health related challenges in a country. The role of the private sector is particularly important in the context of lower and middle-income countries, given the fiscal constraints faced by governments. In addition, a liberal trade policy plays a crucial role for health sector by facilitating exchange of medical services (including doctors and nurses-midwives), FDI in hospitals and medical insurance, freer export and import of medicines etc.

Over the last decade, the health sectors across countries have undergone a number of reform measures. Asian countries have not been an exception to this trend, where both privatization and public-private partnerships (PPPs) have played important roles. Montagu and Bloom (2010) noted the health sector reforms being undertaken in the Easter Asia Pacific region and through case studies covering Cambodia, Philippines, Mongolia, Vietnam, Indonesia and Fiji, have underlined their importance. A series of policy reforms as well as government willingness to partner has helped the private sector to grow in India since 2002 leading to improvements in the health sector (Rao, 2012). IHSD (2004) has also noted the introduction of various schemes involving the private sector in South and Southeast Asia. WHO (2010) noted the country reform experiences and acknowledged the role to be played by the private sector in the South and Southeast Asian countries in ensuring their health security. A similar success resulting from the introduction of the PPP model in Moldova has been reported by IFC (2012). Associated reforms have been equally important as the ICT reforms and enhanced private sector participation has helped the provision of telemedicine in African countries (Kimura et al, undated).

However, problem areas do remain. First and foremost, the reform initiatives have often been incomplete, thereby delivering suboptimal results, which in turn have weakened the hand of reformist policymakers. For instance, Gupta et al (2012) noted that the coverage of the health reforms in emerging economies including the ones in Asia have been incomplete. Second, despite the GATT-WTO reforms dealing with introduction of an international intellectual property regime and the ongoing negotiation on liberalization of health and insurance services and other areas, several concerns continue to surface. To name a few, trade in counterfeit medicines, barriers on movement of medical professionals, services and equipment could be mentioned in this regard.

This volume attempts to explore the present challenges in freeing healthcare services. The book has been divided in two sections. While the first section deals with concerns relating to international trade issues and their health related implications, the second section attempts to explore the recent health reform experiences in several East, Southeast and South Asian countries, with a particular focus on expanding the role of the private sector.

We have selected these regions for focus largely because of the enormous scope for private investment and growth in the health sector, as shown by figures 2 to 7. Figure 1 compares the annual average GDP growth scenario across major regions. It is clearly evident that South, South East and East Asian countries are among the fastest growing regions in the world. While economic growth in many of the MENA countries can be explained by energy product exports, the same for the other two regions can be viewed in the light of their low initial base and increasing liberalization efforts during the last two decades. Since the 1980s several non-market and transition economies in South, South East and East Asia have undertaken reforms, either unilaterally or guided by IMF Structural Adjustment Programmes (SAP) and their GATT-WTO commitments, and their higher growth profile is to some extent indicative of that. Moreover, the markets of high-income countries regions are nearing saturation and hence the growing economies of Asia offer them enormous potentials for returns. Asia on the other hand, stands to gain by accelerating growth rates through enhanced trade, investment and technology collaborations with high-income countries.

While Southeast and East Asia have been able to increase the importance of trade in their economies, South Asia has so far performed relatively poorly on this regard (Figure 3). While the structural compulsions, infrastructural and logistic bottlenecks and several other factors contribute to this situation, insufficient or incomplete trade and industrial policy reforms in these countries are also equally responsible, although in varying degree across South Asian Countries (Gwartney et al, 2012). The health sector is one area that could benefit considerably from future reforms in this region.

While incomplete health sector reforms have weakened private sector performance in several Asian countries, governments have also proved unable to deliver universal access to high-quality, affordable healthcare. Figure 4 shows that average health spending as percentage of government expenditure is lowest in South Asia and has declined marginally over the last decade. On the other hand, the corresponding figure is found to be moderate in Southeast and East Asian countries. As a result, existing health infrastructure in most Asian countries falls short of the required level. It is therefore important to create an environment in which the private sector can deliver extra capacity and thereby contribute towards increasing access to healthcare.

Despite undergoing several decades of robust economic growth, many Asian countries - particularly those in South Asia - are still facing enormous health challenges (Figures 5 to 7). Figure 5 show that average infant mortality rates have improved recently in South and East Asia but South Asia still lags behind. Maternal mortality presents a similar picture (Figure 6). Finally, Figure 7 shows the incidence of TB cases across continents over the last two decades. East Asia and the Pacific and South Asia still suffer high rates of this ancient scourge, even in this new millennium. The second part of this volume looks at way in which the private sector can contribute to reversing this situation.

Figure 2: Average Annual GDP Growth Rate (%)

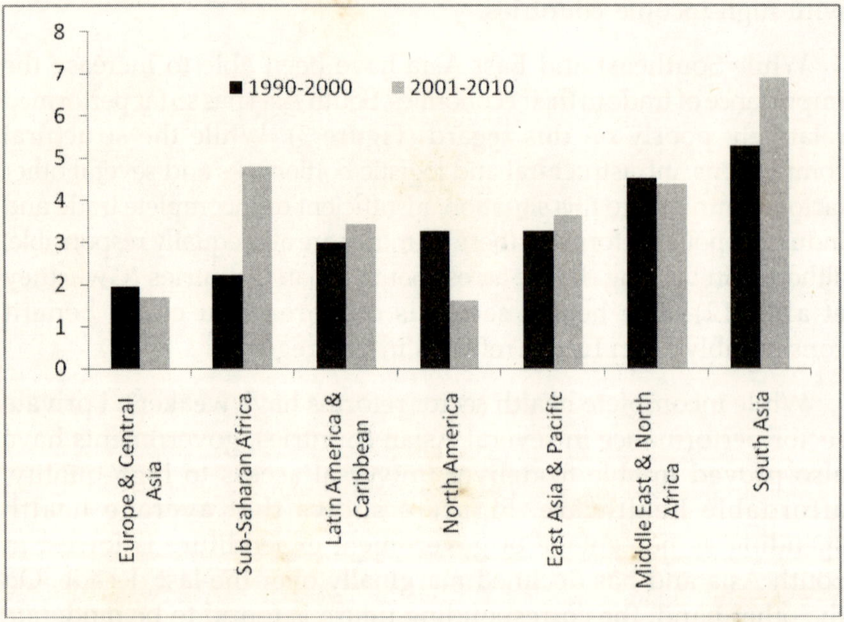

Source: Constructed from the World Development Indicators Data

Figure 3: Average Exports of goods and services (% of GDP)

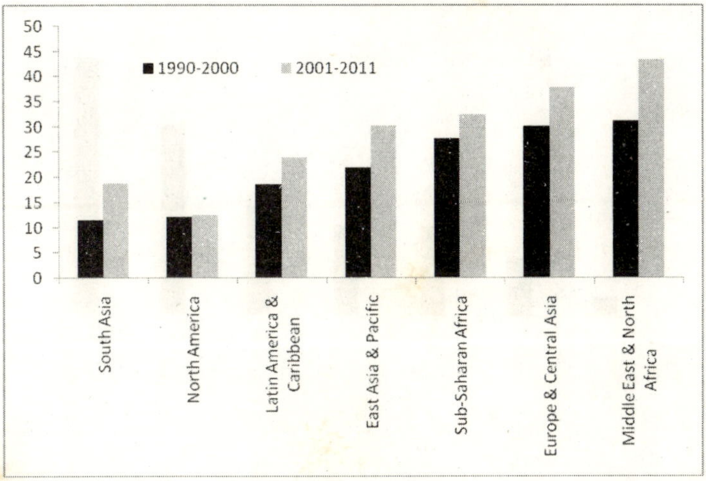

Source: Constructed from the World Development Indicators Data

Figure 4: Average Health expenditure, public (% of government expenditure)

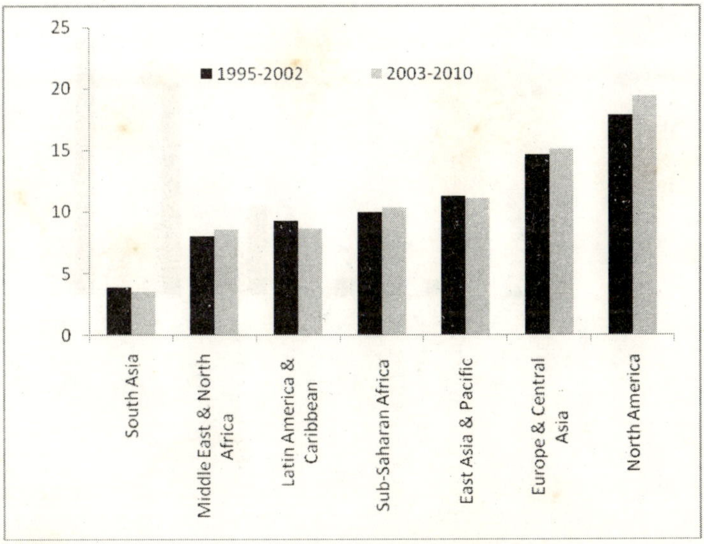

Source: Constructed from the World Development Indicators Data

Figure 5: Average Mortality rate, infant (per 1,000 live births)

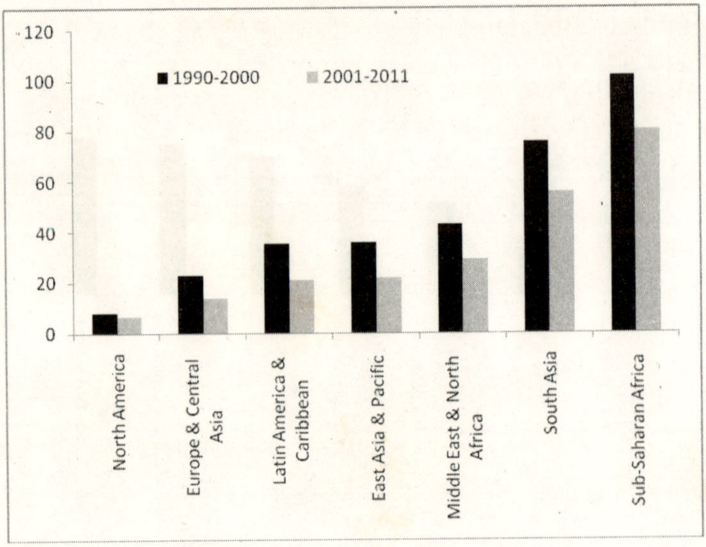

Source: Constructed from the World Development Indicators Data

Figure 6: Average Number of maternal deaths (per 1000)

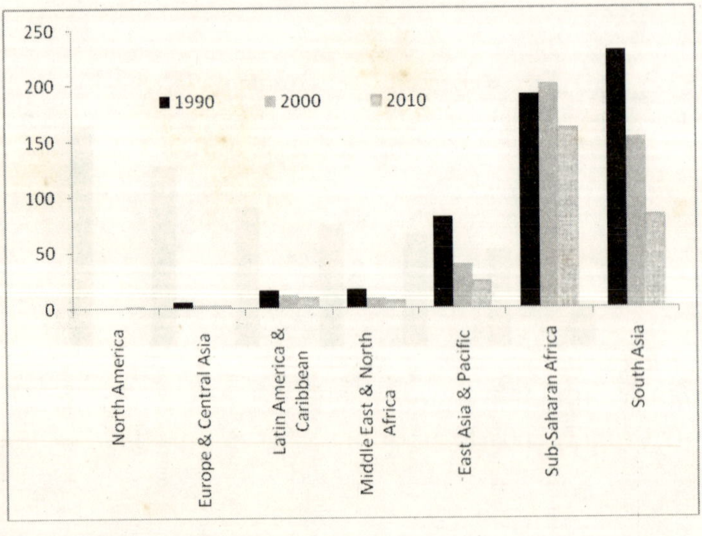

Source: Constructed from the World Development Indicators Data

Figure 7: Incidence of tuberculosis (per 100,000 people)

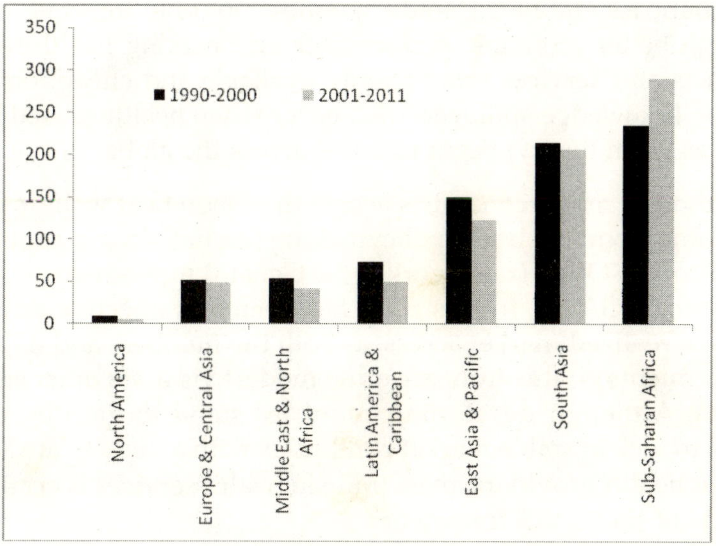

Source: Constructed from the World Development Indicators Data

The Volume

The first chapter by Philip Stevens provides an overview of the various mechanisms through which free trade - driven by tariff reductions and import / export liberalisation leads to improvements in health. During the middle of the Twentieth Century the world witnessed a rise of Import-Substituting Industrialization (ISI) policies, which merely led to temporary rise in industrial output at the cost of agricultural output. This caused an unavoidable injection of subsidies into globally uncompetitive industries, and resulting debt and inflation spirals. Since the 1990s the GATT-WTO reforms as well as macroeconomic imperatives have led to trade and industrial policy reforms, thereby setting the stage for rapid economic growth and deepening integration in the global economy. Increased trade openness has considerably influenced health across countries, particularly in the lower income ones. During the second half of the twentieth century, lower-income countries saw their life-expectancies rise rapidly as incomes rose and new technology arrived from overseas – lowering the costs of trade can speed up the rate at which proven medical technologies can be adopted by other countries. The analysis concludes by noting that countries embracing trade openness not only improve health through better economic performance and making health-related products and services more readily available and cheap, but also via the 'knowledge spillovers' that occur when health-related ideas (such as germ theory) begin to travel across the globe.

Although most economists accept the theoretical welfare gains that come from free trade, policymaking has not always kept pace. The 'Request-Offer' framework in the General Agreement on Trade in Services (GATS), for instance, has been less effective so far in terms of realized market access, as both the numbers and depth of commitments on this front are quite modest vis-à-vis other service sectors. Although developing countries stand to gain by using GATS to lock in stable market conditions with a view to attracting foreign health providers, most trade in health services is occurring outside of the GATS framework.

Fredrik Erixon in the second chapter notes that despite the enormous potential to drive up quality and improve efficiency presented by international trade in healthcare, it remains a marginal phenomenon bereft of a real systematic trade policy. The analysis sets out the lukewarm reception of the liberalization opportunity presented by GATS by the historically ingrained regulatory restrictions and institutional constraints that exist in domestic healthcare sectors, reflecting traditional views of healthcare and preventing cross-border movement of services. The chapter argues that the basic opposition of undertaking healthcare reform through trade negotiations is based on normative arguments like the "fundamental human right" of populations to healthcare and the perceived inherent difference of interest between profit-making businesses and those of society at large etc. The complex relationship is clearly visible for advanced developing countries like Brazil, India, and Thailand; while on one hand they promote export strategies for facilitating "healthcare tourism", fairly high tariffs for medicaments and health-related products protect their domestic players on the other.

Persistence of these 'semi-protectionisms' in several economies is indeed harmful for another reason. The evidence from literature strongly indicates that appropriate protection of intellectual property rights (IPRs) can facilitate knowledge and technology diffusion in middle and lower-income countries through increased trade in goods and services, foreign direct investment, joint ventures, licensing etc. IPRs can promote knowledge diffusion in healthcare, as the information available in patent claims is publically available, and therefore easily accessible by other potential inventors who can use that information to invent around the patent to make improvements and modifications. However, 'public interest' groups have opposed international intellectual property regimes on the basis that they restrict access to the poor by driving up prices of medicines. The third chapter by Philip Stevens argues that such concerns are often misplaced, as around 98 per cent of drugs on the World Health Organization's Essential Medicines List are off-patent. Discussions on this front finally led to the 2001 'Doha Declaration' at the WTO Doha Ministerial, which inserted a number of flexibilities into the TRIPs agreement by recognizing the gravity of the public health problems affecting developing countries. In reality, access to medical technologies in lower income countries is not so much a product of intellectual property laws, but rather a range of other factors including: the absorptive capacities of local industries and businesses; physical infrastructure; stable macroeconomic and political environment; restrictions on inward technology; trade and investment flows; regulatory systems etc.

The inability of countries to effectively enforce a strong IP regime is responsible for existence of a sizable global trade in fake medicines, which continues to grow. Trade in fake medicines results in millions of people unwittingly consuming adulterated substances (e.g. cement, talcum powder, sawdust, paint and an array of other toxic or inert substances), and fake medicines represent up to a third of medicines in some poor countries, most notably in Africa. This thwarts efforts to cure disease, worsens illness and results in the emergence of drug resistant strains of diseases such as tuberculosis and malaria. The fourth chapter by

Julian Morris, Julian Harris and Philip Stevens reports that resistance is currently a serious problem with tuberculosis, as stronger, deadlier mutations emerge such as the XDR-TB strain (Extremely Drug Resistant Tuberculosis), now confirmed in 49 countries ranging from Peru to Nepal. Widespread resistance is also a very serious problem with malaria. Fake medicines also weaken the pharmaceutical sector by affecting spending on research and development (R&D) into new medicines. The problem persists given the presence of several problems in low-income countries, including: defective legal systems; absent or defective trademark protection; inability to resolve disputes over property rights and contracts in independent courts; weak or absent rule of law; tariffs and other import restrictions; price controls etc. The analysis recommended strengthening of local institutions (in particular those related to the rule of law) and creating an environment in which brand-owners can protect their products.

India maintained a stronger IPR regime in the pre-independence period, but subsequently a process patent regime was adopted by policymakers citing public health concerns. While the policy helped the domestic pharmaceutical sector to grow by reverse engineering of patented medicines, the industry remained very low value-added, spending very little on R & D. Subsequently, the country had to move to product patent regime in the post-WTO period, after conceding defeat on this front at WTO Dispute Settlement Body. In the following period, India joined hands with several developing countries and LDCs for modification of the TRIPS provisions through incorporation of parallel import and compulsory licensing provisions, on the ground of public health concerns.

Although the Doha Declaration (2001) was a major negotiating success for these economies, the welfare implications are dubious. The fifth chapter by Amir Ullah Khan notes that both compulsory licensing and parallel imports are emerging as causes of concern in the Indian context. The Indian law on patents allows compulsory licensing when "the patented invention is not available to the public at an affordable and reasonable price". The analysis reports the case of Natco Pharmaceuticals in India which has been granted a compulsory license to manufacture and sell the cancer drug Nexavar that belonged to Bayer, after payment of a 6% royalty to the MNC. However, the author notes that the new price proposed by Natco is by no means affordable to poor patients from India whom this policy is ostensibly designed to serve. The analysis argues that in a country like India, which already suffers from a track record of weak IPR, such developments will only make foreign investors wary of coming to India - and neither will it address the true causes of poor health, which relate to sanitation, malnutrition and weak health infrastructure.

As populations in middle and low-income countries become wealthier as a result of globalisation and economic liberalisation, many governments are now placing an increased focus on improving the provision of social welfare services such as health and education. This drive to achieve "Universal Healthcare" is often led by government, with countries such as India envisaging a stronger role for the state both in the provision and financing of services. This state-centric approach invites skepticism, as most Ministries of Health in Asian countries do not have the capacity, expertise, logistical skills, or incentives to deliver a complex service like healthcare to every citizen. In particular, countries characterized by weak rule of law has been susceptible to corruptions at many levels, including direct embezzlement at the ministerial level; fraud in billing; local medical staff selling "free" drugs on the grey market, institutionalised absenteeism etc. The failures are not always attributable to weaknesses within the public sector *per se*, but to the misalignment of incentives faced by centralized public health bureaucracies, leading to unresponsive to local demand, lack of direct accountability, possibilities of rent-seeking activities etc. The sixth chapter by Philip Stevens examines models of private sector experimentation for healthcare provision in several countries. The analysis covers both supply-side models (social franchising, contracting, PPPs, pure private provision) which involve the private sector delivering health services to patients, and demand-side interventions (health equity funds, microfinance / community health insurance, Private health insurance), which increase the ability of patients to access those services. The latter mechanisms include methods of funding access to health services on behalf of patients, particularly the poorest. The analysis notes the ability of operators to innovate and experiment in order to bring costs down while expanding services. While government role in setting standards and monitoring quality is acknowledged, the evidence suggests that private providers need to be granted managerial autonomy if they are to function effectively in wider health systems.

Access to quality healthcare for low-income groups has remained a priority for governments and donors working in developing countries alike. Although a wide range of services are available to the general public, the gap especially with regard to the accessibility of health services for low-income groups such as labourers, minorities, domestic workers, and street vendors is still considerable. Healthcare in Pakistan has undergone many changes over the last thirty years, moving from a largely curative approach to one based more on primary health care (i.e. focus on prevention) and also being guided by the MDGs. The seventh chapter by Mehreen Zahid Malik and Ali Salman reviews practices in provision of health vouchers in India, Kenya, Nicaragua, Uganda and Taiwan so as to determine how they might be adapted to Pakistan. The review notes that in general there is a focus on either maternal health or reproductive health. In light of the international experiences, the analysis recommends their implementation in Pakistan with certain modifications, e.g. launching of promotional and awareness campaign to reach target beneficiaries, incorporating a transport stipend in areas characterized by poor mobility, using market based services as a benchmark for pricing a voucher, providing some preferences to more prevalent diseases or health related problems pertaining to specific location etc. However, the study strongly underlines the need to sort out several key issues (e.g. identification of priority package of health services to be provided, cost-effectiveness, pricing, distribution, characteristics, monitoring and evaluating effectiveness, risks, misuse, and remedial strategies) before designing such a health voucher scheme.

A driving objective of the policymakers in Philippines is to provide universal healthcare to each of the citizens in line with the prevalent model in European and North American countries, where government takes the dominant role in the healthcare system, and most costs are underwritten by the public purse. While the budgetary allocation to the Health departments as well as spending is on the rise, this is not sustainable as the Philippine government is still heavily indebted. Although there are several hundred private hospitals, the government continues to be the main supplier of healthcare services nationwide. The eighth chapter by Bienvenido "Nonoy" Oplas, Jr. notes that the country has witnessed improvement in health indicators but with fluctuations and analyzes the reforms undertaken in the sector. For patients brought to private hospital emergency rooms (ERs), financing for outpatient services is usually administered via Health Maintenance Organizations (HMOs), Local Government Units (LGUs), and Out-of-Pocket (OOP) for those who have no private health insurance or LGU health card. The present condition is highly disadvantageous to the poor because of the huge out of pocket expenses. The argument is that for achieving UHC, PhilHealth (the government's social insurance fund) needs to be reformed into a more centralised agency with much wider coverage and services. This proposal is most likely inappropriate for a country such as the Philippines, which is characterized by a weak rule of law and highly politicized culture and greater involvement may not necessarily lead to UHC. The paper concludes by suggesting that the government's role in healthcare be limited to the areas where it has comparative advantage, such as: standard setting, regulation, dealing with infectious or communicable diseases, pediatric diseases, and children and adults with physical or mental limitations etc. This would generate greater competition above the services that PhilHealth will not cover – like outpatient services, diagnostic tests, annual general check-up, and dental services, and the resulting expansion of choice for citizens will improve welfare.

The ninth chapter by Yu Hui and colleagues discusses some of the structural problems with Chinese healthcare, many of which revolve around the fact that state-provided services have been captured by political elites. As a result, public services are neither available nor affordable, and a booming black market has developed to gain access to public facilities. Hence, the majority of Chinese population rely on unqualified or unguaranteed medical services in private hospitals. Although private hospitals have their advantages, for instance, in terms of the ownership and governance structure, they face a number of weaknesses, many of which derive from an anti-competitive and distorted legislative and regulatory environment. These constraints are hampering their growth and their ability to contribute to equitable and high quality healthcare for all Chinese, which is the stated view of the Chinese government. This essay analyses some of the problems facing the private hospital sector, and sets out some possible ideas for reform.

India along with China is the only other country that has witnessed a consistent annual average GDP growth rate of over 7 percent during the last decade. The healthcare industry in India has emerged as a major segment of the economy, with a growth rate of more than 13 per cent per annum during this period. A slide up the value chain by major players has enabled India to emerge as a prominent destination for medical tourism. Policymakers, meanwhile, have realized the limitations of the public sector framework in providing universal healthcare, given the huge population size. Given the expertise and capacity that is undoubtedly possessed by the private sector, the government has been keen to develop innovative public private partnerships (PPPs) to help improve healthcare for the poor. However, these reforms have been embarked on half-heartedly in many cases, and there needs to be a change of mind-set from the government if they are to be effective. The last chapter by Debashis Chakraborty analyzes the existing healthcare sector scenario in India in the light of these ongoing PPP reforms and their effects. Taking note of the shortfall in existing public-sector infrastructure, the analysis attempts to understand how far recent reforms have been able to attract private companies into the health sector. While the National Rural Health Mission (NRHM) and National Urban Health Mission (NUHM) of the government attempts to secure synergies with the private sector through PPPs, their effectiveness so far has been weakened by a wider set of factors including hasty planning; mismatch between grassroot needs and government agenda; untimely budgetary devolution from the government; greater emphasis on achieving the quantitative target, rather than ensuring the quality of the service; political interference; government inefficiency and red tape; and failure to devise sufficient in-built incentives etc. The paper concludes by stressing the need to undertake the unfinished reforms.

Bibliography

Gupta, Sanjeev, Benedict Clements, and David Coady (2012), "The Challenge of Health Care Reform in Advanced and Emerging Economies", in Benedict Clements, David Coady and Sanjeev Gupta (Eds.), *The economics of public health care reform in advanced and emerging economies*, International Monetary Fund, Washington, DC.

Gwartney, James and Robert Lawson and Joshua Hall (2012), "Economic Freedom of the World: 2012 Annual Report", Fraser Institute, Vancouver.

Institute for Health Sector Development (2004), "Private Sector Participation in Health", London.

International Finance Corporation (2012), "Moldova: Radiology and Diagnostic Imaging Center", Success Stories - Public Private Partnerships series, Washington DC.

Kimura, Kaoru, Duncan Wambogo Omole, and Mark Williams (undated), "ICT in Sub-Saharan Africa: Success Stories", available at http://siteresources.worldbank.org/AFRICAEXT/Resources/258643-1271798012256/ICT-19.pdf (last accessed on November 22, 2012).

Kumaranayake, Lilani (1997), "The Role of Regulation: Influencing Private Sector activity within Health Sector Reform", *Journal of International Development*, 9(4): 641-649.

Miller, Terry, Kim R. Holmes and Edwin J. Feulner (2012), "Highlights of the 2012 Index of Economic Freedom: Promoting Economic Opportunity and Prosperity", Heritage Foundation in partnership with the Wall Street Journal.

Montagu, Dominic and Abby Bloom (2010), "The Private Sector and Health Services Delivery in the EAP Region: Background Report to UNICEF on the Role and Experiences of the Private Sector in Provision of Child Health Services", UNICEF.

Rao, P. H. (2012), "The Private Health Sector in India: A Framework for Improving the Quality of Care", *ASCI Journal of Management*, 41 (2): 14–39.

United Nations Conference on Trade and Development (2011), "Poverty Reduction and Progress towards MDGs in the LDCs: Encouraging Signs but Much Remains to be done", UNCTAD Policy Brief No. 20, Least developed Countries Series, Geneva.

World Health Organization (2010), "Health-Care Reform for the Twenty-first Century in the South-East Asia Region", Report of the Regional Meeting Bangkok, Thailand, 20-22 October 2009, WHO Regional Office for South-East Asia, New Delhi.

Wu, Xun and M. Ramesh (2009), "Health Care Reforms in Developing Asia: Propositions and Realities", *Development and Change*, 40(3): 531–549.

1

The Globalization of Health: Open Trade and The Diffusion of Health Technology, Knowledge and Wealth

Philip Stevens[1]

Introduction

The history of humanity shows that the most certain and sustainable way of improving human health is to increase individual prosperity and wealth. A seminal 1996 study by economists Lant Pritchett and Lawrence Summers showed the dramatic effect that increases in incomes have on health. They found a strong causative effect of income on infant mortality, and demonstrated that if the developing world's growth rate had been 1.5 percentage points higher in the 1980s, half a million infant deaths would have been averted.

Wealth alone is not enough: knowledge and the spread of that knowledge are essential. Some of the most potent health-promoting things known to man - germ theory, vaccination, sewerage - are simply ideas that have spread around the world. But these ideas need economic resources to make a difference; sewage systems are expensive, for example, as are mass vaccination programmes or the construction of hygienic dwellings.

But much of this economic growth and diffusion of health knowledge could never have been achieved without the dramatic increases in international trade that characterised the late nineteenth century and second half of the twentieth century. Before the late nineteenth century, cross-border trade was confined to handful of nations. Today, all countries trade internationally and, with the occasional exception such as North Korea, they trade significant - and increasing - proportions of their national incomes. It would not be hyperbolic to say that the rise of international trade over the last 120 years has brought modern medicine and public health to almost every corner of the planet, bringing with it a revolution in global life expectancies and living standards. Without trade, life would still be nasty, brutish and short for the vast majority of humanity - as it has been throughout human history, with the exception of the last century.

This chapter provides an overview of the various mechanisms through which free trade - driven by tariff reductions and import/ export liberalisation - improves health. Given that tariffs have largely been removed over several decades of multilateral and unilateral action on trade, the chapter concludes with an analysis of a more contemporary concern: the introduction of 'beyond the border' measures such as Intellectual Property Requirements in modern trade regimes, and their impact on health.

Barriers to open markets

Lower-income countries have been able to begin to participate successfully in global markets, partly through abandoning the old protectionist policies of the post-war period. Chief among these was Import-substitution industrialisation (ISI), which was promoted very widely after World War II and was implemented aggressively and enthusiastically in many lower-income countries, especially in post-independence Africa.

The justifications for ISI policies were twofold. Firstly, it was taken as a given that development required industrialisation. Secondly, it was supposed that governments could speed this process up by preventing imports of industrial goods - thereby encouraging the development of a local industry.

Following the advice of proponents of ISI, Brazil and other Latin American economies put massive restrictions - quotas, tariffs, and outright bans - on imports of industrial goods. As a result, there was a temporary rise in industrial output. This is not surprising: if you restrict the import of goods that people have traditionally imported, then local production will compensate to some extent.

However, the initial cost was a reduction in agricultural output, as productive factors moved into industry and away from agriculture, and as people migrated from the countryside into the cities. After a period of time, industrial output began to level off, mainly because the output was no longer competitive. As it was no longer possible to purchase essential productive inputs from abroad, efficiency of outputs was constrained. The costs of inputs rose and so competitors overseas did better.

To save the industries that had been sponsored by import-substitution policies, governments started to subsidise them. To pay for these subsidies, they raised taxes on agriculture and monetised government debt through inflation. The net result was hyper-inflation, combined with unemployment and negative growth.

In addition, it created social chaos. This is because many people had migrated to towns and were now unemployed. If they had been unemployed in the countryside, they would have had their social support networks that had been developed over decades. But the new migrants to towns had not developed such networks.

Open trade improves health

Fortunately, by the close of the Uruguay Round of GATT negotiations in 1994, most countries had agreed to move away from this counterproductive strategy and lower significantly their protectionist tariffs. In many countries, this set the stage for rapid economic growth and deepening integration in the global economy.

As well as being a period of increasing global trade and economic activity, the second half of the twentieth century also saw remarkable improvements in health inmost lower-income countries. Between 1950 and 2003, for example, India's infant mortality fell from 190to 63 per 1,000. In fact, life expectancy in low and middle-income countries has risen steadily since the middle of the twentieth century, with the exception of sub-Saharan Africa and Russia in the 1990s. This progress took place against a backdrop of increasing international trade.

Can any link be drawn between the increasing global importance of trade and improving health in the developing world? There appear to be two main mechanisms through which trade liberalisation improves health: first, and most obviously, via the increases in incomes that arise from increased openness to trade; and secondly, via the global diffusion of knowledge that has accompanied greater economic globalisation and trade liberalisation. These two hypotheses are examined in the following section.

Trade, wealth and health

The health of the world's population has been improving since modern economic growth began with the Industrial Revolution. Infant mortality and life expectancy rates have improved dramatically around the world, as increasing numbers of people abandon the precarious subsistence agrarian lives of their forebears, and gain access to increasingly cheap food, better accommodation and improved public health and sanitary infrastructure, often in towns and cities. Basic health indicators improved noticeably in rich countries from the mid to late nineteenth century as nations cleaned up their water supplies and instituted basic public health measures, such as sanitation, pasteurisation, and vaccination. Then, in the first half of the twentieth century, antibiotics, pesticides such as DDT, and an array of vaccines were added to the arsenal of weapons against disease. Once the traditional infectious and parasitic diseases were essentially conquered, richer countries turned their ingenuity and wealth to dealing with the increasing burden of non-communicable diseases such as heart disease, cancer and pulmonary conditions. While these have not yet been entirely defeated, a vast array of new treatments, drugs and technologies now exist to mitigate their effects and in some cases, cure.

Much of this economic growth and diffusion of health knowledge could never have been achieved without the dramatic increases in international trade that characterised the late nineteenth century and the second half of the twentieth century. Before the late nineteenth century, cross-border trade was confined to a handful of nations. Today, all countries trade internationally and, with the occasional exception such as North Korea, they trade significant – and increasing – proportions of their national incomes. While higher-income countries still accounted for three quarters of global trade in 2000, lower-income countries have recently seen their share climb by one third as they have cut tariffs and dismantled other barriers to free trade. The average tariff in lower-income countries has fallen from 25 per cent in the late 1980s to 11 per cent today (World Bank and IMF, 2005). According to the WTO, lower-income countries now command 31 per cent of global merchandise trade, their highest level since the 1950s (WTO, 2005).

This relatively recent entry by developing countries into global markets has had an astonishing impact on human welfare. During the second half of the twentieth century, lower-income countries saw their life-expectancies rise rapidly as incomes rose and new technology arrived from overseas, described by Gwatkin (1980) as the third of three great waves of mortality decline. This period saw increased access to safe water and sanitation services in lower-income countries, increases in per capita food supplies, the arrival of basic public health services, greater knowledge of basic hygiene, and new medical technologies (such as antibiotics and tests for early diagnosis) that were instrumental in reducing mortality rates. As a result of these advances, life expectancies lengthened worldwide, not just in the richest nations. Average global life expectancy increased from 46.6 years between1950–1955 to 69.2 in 2009, as increased wealth and knowledge spread around the world.

Trade, knowledge spill-overs and health

Increased openness to trade, then, is clearly one determinant of the income of a country, and income obviously has a bearing on health status. However, a less obvious relationship between trade and health is not so much economic, but rather related to 'knowledge spill-overs' that occur as people, goods and technologies move more freely around the world. The notion that these exchanges of ideas have been instrumental to improving health in developing countries is shared both by Owen and Wu's 2007 analysis of the relationship between trade and health; and Jamison, Sandbu and Wang in their 2001 analysis prepared for the WHO's Commission on Macroeconomics and Health.

Knowledge spill-overs are an intrinsic outcome of increased international trade. When the costs of trade are lowered, it becomes easier to disseminate to other countries the knowledge, techniques and medical products from the countries that developed them. This knowledge can have a profound impact on health outcomes. For example, the discovery by John Snow in London in 1854 that cholera is spread by contaminated water had significant implications for the prevention of infectious diseases throughout the world. This knowledge gradually filtered from London throughout Europe, where other scientists built upon it and developed more refined and applicable knowledge regarding the role of microbes in the spread of disease. This diffusion of knowledge led city authorities to upgrade their water and sewage systems in order to prevent human waste contaminating water supplies (Williamson, 1990). Today, germ theory is widely understood and recognised by public health authorities all over the world as an important tool for fighting disease, with even the poorest countries recognising that sanitation infrastructure is vital for population health (even if the resources do not always exist to construct and maintain effective water management systems). Germ theory was only the beginning; today the health consequences of over-eating, smoking, excessive drinking and inactivity are well known amongst medical professionals the world over. This knowledge is at the centre of today's attempts to tackle the rising incidence of chronic diseases in less-developed countries (WHO, 2011), even though the research which originally gave rise to this knowledge was originally largely conducted in wealthy countries.

Similarly, lowering the costs of trade can speed up the rate at which proven medical technologies can be adopted by other countries. Some of the most effective medicines such as antibiotics and vaccines were first developed in richer countries, but the international manufacture and trade of such technologies has allowed them to become readily available in most parts of the world.

The 1920s to 1940s saw huge advances and discoveries in medical science, including penicillin, sulfa drugs, bacitracin, streptomycin and chloroquine. In the post-war years,. with the arrival in Asia of these and other drugs, effective treatments became available at low cost and are largely responsible for the remarkable declines in their crude death rates. In the 1940s, Asia ended several decades of relative economic and cultural isolation, and started to integrate into the global economy. This brought with it a massive transfer and diffusion of public health programmes, technologies and techniques that originated in richer countries. Furthermore, the invention of DDT in 1943 gave authorities a hugely powerful weapon in the fight against malaria which allowed the disease to be eradicated from the US and Europe, and to lower caseloads by over 99 per cent in parts of Sri Lanka and India (Gramiccia and Beales, 1988).

As a result of the widening availability and decreasing cost of such interventions -made possible by freer trade - crude death rates dropped steeply, particularly in eastern Asia in the late 1940s. By the 1950s and 1960s, fewer and fewer children and young people were succumbing to the easily preventable diseases which had historically depressed the region's health indicators, and life expectancy was on the rise throughout the region (Bloom and Williamson, 1998).

This process continues today. New drugs and medicines invented in one place are made available elsewhere, throughout the world, via international markets. Nearly all drugs start off protected by patents, but these eventually expire, opening the market for generic competition. As a result, many off-patent medicines are available throughout the world at extremely low prices – allowing people in poorer countries to benefit from the knowledge and innovation of more affluent countries. Recent examples of this include antiretroviral drugs, statins and insulin, as well as neonatal intensive care units, kidney dialysis equipment, screening equipment and myriad other modern medical devices. The year 2011 saw the expiry of the patent of atorvastatin. This means that this highly effective statin is now open to generic competition.

Countries such as India are exploiting their low-cost, high-skill comparative advantage to manufacture cheap generic versions of the drug, and leveraging their global supply chains to sell their products in markets ranging from Kenya to the United States. None of this would be possible without international trade, both in terms of the ability to move goods across borders to global markets, and having access to the knowledge and skills to reverse engineer a branded medicine in the first place. Of course, many on-patent drugs are subject to competition from other medicines in the same class which place downward pressure on price. Moreover, with price differentiation, on-patent drugs may be made available to poorer people at prices close to the cost of production, an increasingly prevalent marketing strategy amongst drug manufacturers (Yadav, 2010). Again, a necessary precondition to effective competition is the ability to trade across borders.

Free Trade Agreements

A recurring theme of the related literature is that bilateral Free Trade Agreements are harmful to health because of the inclusion of mandatory intellectual property provisions by the economically stronger negotiating partner (typically the US or European Union). The imposition of strict intellectual property regimes on lower and middle-income countries, so the argument goes, is deleterious to health because it reduces generic competition and drives up the price of medicines and other patented health technologies (Shaffer and Brennan, 2009; Aziz ur Rehmana, 2010). This form of criticism is not new, having been around since intellectual property provisions were first included in the Uruguay Round negotiations of the GATT and, later, the World Trade Organization in the form of the 1994 TRIPs agreement. Specific research claims to have found that Free Trade Agreements have reduced access to certain medicines in Guatemala (via CAFTA) (Shaffer and Brennan, 2009) and in Jordan (Oxfam, 2007). This debate has recently been reignited by the European Union's negotiation of a bilateral agreement with India, as well as the on-going multilateral negotiations of the Trans Pacific Partnership, involving the US and a range of countries from the Asia Pacific region (see for example, MSF, 2011).

While theoretically plausible, there is no analysis that demonstrates that the arrival of the international intellectual property regime in the mid-1990s through the WTO resulted in an average decrease in health outcomes, as would be expected if such criticisms were valid. On the contrary, life expectancies continued to rise until 1995 in all countries following the creation of the TRIPs agreement in 1994, although certain global events (for instance the HIV pandemic and the dissolution of the Soviet Union) exerted downward regional pressure on health indicators in the same period. Even so, over this period, average life expectancy rose worldwide, and rapidly so in lower-income countries.

What, then, of the oft-heard criticisms that Free Trade Agreements undermine health by reducing access to medicines in developing countries because of unnecessarily strict intellectual property regimes? The reality is that intellectual property is somewhat of a peripheral concern when it comes to healthcare in the poorest countries. A 2004 study by Amir Attaran found that 98 per cent of drugs on the World Health Organization's Essential Medicines List are off-patent. Many of the biggest killers of children in low-income countries – diarrhoea and respiratory infections – are easily preventable or treatable with cheap, off-patent medicines. Yet, according to the WHO, an estimated 30 per cent of the world's population lacks regular access to existing drugs, with this figure rising to over 50 per cent in the poorest parts of Africa and Asia (WHO, 2004). The majority of non-communicable diseases can be treated or managed with off-patent therapies, but access to these medicines in lower-income countries remains low (WHO, 2011). Many modern patented cancer and biotech therapies require complex delivery and monitoring systems that are simply not available in lower and middle-income countries. The evidence therefore suggests that it is not necessarily patents that block access to thousands of useful therapies, but other factors relating to the supply chain and infrastructure. As such, the inclusion of intellectual property provisions in Free Trade Agreements is by itself unlikely to have either a positive or negative impact on overall population health.

Some activist groups assert that certain intellectual property provisions in Free Trade Agreements (the Trans Pacific Partnership being most current) will prevent countries from making use of safeguards provided in the Doha Declaration on the TRIPS Agreement and Public Health. Signed by all WTO member countries, the declaration restated flexibilities in TRIPS that allow countries to take necessary measures, including the compulsory licensing of medicines, to protect public health. A further clarification in August 2003 ensured that third-party countries could also compulsory-license drugs for export to poor countries lacking manufacturing capability.

When campaigning against Free Trade Agreements, activist groups also raise the spectre of patent terms that go beyond the TRIPS' minimum of 20 years, thus suggesting a situation where poor people would have to wait 20 years or more before they can get access to generic drugs.[2] But, as we have seen, 98 per cent of drugs on the World Health Organization's essential drugs list are off-patent and will remain so (Attaran, 2004). Similarly, drugs patented in the US but not in other countries, including many antiretrovirals, cannot gain patent protection now. In any case, no drugs have a *de facto* 20-year patent term. It typically takes between 10 and 12 years to take a molecule through testing and regulatory approval – all of which occur after a patent has been granted, since no company would invest in an unpatented molecule. Meanwhile, it can take between one and three years to obtain a patent after filing. Therefore, most drugs have an effective patent term of six to ten years, often less.

According to the US Food and Drug Administration (FDA), the average patent life remaining after marketing approval in 2001 was 7.8 years out of the original 20 years of patent protection (FDA, 2002). By contrast, other industrial sectors enjoy an average patent life of more than 18.5 years. Some Free Trade Agreements do provide for patent term restoration, but only in the case of unnecessary delays in marketing approvals. In the US, where such legislation exists, this extra term typically does not exceed two years. Marketing approval in lower-income countries can take many years, due to delays and bottlenecks in poorly resourced local drug regulatory authorities. In South Africa, for example, these delays can delay the marketing approval of new medicines by up to five years.[3] In other words, most drugs would still have far less than 20 years of exclusivity.

Concerns have also been raised about the inclusion of new Data Exclusivity requirements in Free Trade Agreements. When submitting a new product to regulators for marketing approval, manufacturers are required to also submit the data generated during clinical trials. Data Exclusivity is a form of Intellectual Property that allows manufacturers to retain the right to this valuable data, preventing competitors from using it until that period elapses. While the standard has been five years for most Free Trade Agreements, the TPP is likely to introduce 12 years of Data Exclusivity for "biosimilar" drugs (generic copies of biotech drugs), thereby bringing negotiating partners into line with US law. Arguments for this extra period of exclusivity have centred on the recent narrowing of patents for biotech products, making it easier for competitors to invent around an on-patent innovator product.

For developing countries, such arguments are again somewhat peripheral to the question of technology transfer. Given that many modern biologic drugs require complex delivery mechanisms and close medical supervision (for example Humira for Crohns disease, or Herceptin for breast cancer), lower-income countries with anything less than extremely modern health facilities cannot take advantage of these medicines, even if they were given away for free. As such, it is difficult to see how Data Exclusivity requirements in Free Trade Agreements can have any meaningful impact on health outcomes in developing countries.

Undoubtedly, Free Trade Agreements are a second-best solution to multilateral free trade. Nevertheless, they are an improvement on past arrangements, freeing up trade and improving economic wellbeing. This allows countries to spend more on healthcare, as well as enabling individuals to improve their living conditions and thus improve health.

Conclusion

Countries that embrace free trade and reject import substitution policies will not only improve health through better economic performance, but will make it possible for consumers to acquire higher quality, less expensive goods that contribute to human health.

Mortality and morbidity in lower-income countries, for example, are greatly increased by the indoor air pollution that arises from burning primitive biomass fuels such as cow dung. Free trade would make imported, cleaner fuels such as gas and kerosene cheaper and more readily available, and would indirectly pressure governments to reform their energy sectors.

Similarly, a large part of the disease burden in the poorest countries is directly attributable to dirty water, so free trade in water purification and related technologies would be also extremely beneficial. Finally, free trade in foodstuffs would allow a far better match between supply and demand than is currently the case in many parts of the world, and would help combat malnutrition - a significant determinant of health. This is particularly true of many African countries, who needlessly erect swingeing tariff barriers between themselves in order to protect their local agricultural sectors.

However, the knowledge spill-overs discussed in this paper would be more potent if there were greater international trade in healthcare. New developments such as telemedicine and medical tourism would particularly benefit developing countries, as would the freer international movement of medical professionals for overseas training and practice. Telemedicine has particular potential, given its ability to reduce costs and deliver expertise rapidly to rural areas that are typically under-served by medical services. Hospital and clinical management could also benefit from the increased innovation and productivity gains that could emerge from exposure to international competition. However, there is little international trade in healthcare services, even though mechanisms exist via the World Trade Organization's General Agreement on Trade in Services, as Fredrik Erixon discusses in his chapter in this volume. To improve the health of the world's people, more free trade is needed - not less.

Notes

1 Executive Director, Emerging Markets Health Network.

2 See, for example: Medicins Sans Frontieres, Sept 2011, "How the Trans Pacific Partnership Threatens Access to Medicines", TPP Issue Brief.

3 "Medicines Control Council to address drug registration delays", *Pharma and Healthcare Insight,* September 2009, available at http://www.pharmaceuticalsinsight.com/file/99346/medicines-control-council-to-address-drug-registration-delays.html.

Bibliography

Aziz ur Rehmana, H, (2010), "India, TRIPS-plus free trade agreements and the future of access to essential medicines. *Information & Communications Technology Law,* 19(3): 267-300.

Bloom, D., & Williamson, J., (1997), "Demographic change and human resource development", In Asian Development Bank, *Emerging Asia,* Manila.

Cornia, G, Rosignoli, S, Tiberti L. (2007), "Globalisation and health: impact pathways and recent evidence" Center for Global, International and Regional Studies. Mapping global inequalities: conference papers (paper mgi-7). http://repositories.cdlib.org/cgirs/mgi/mgi-7.

Dollar, D., & Kraay, A., (2001), *Trade, growth, and poverty,* Policy Research Working Paper No 2199, Washington DC: World Bank.

Dollar, D., (1992), "Outward-oriented developing countries really do grow more rapidly: evidence from 95 LDCs, 1976–85", *Economic Development and Cultural Change*, 40(3): 523–44.

Frankel, J., & Romer, D., (1999), "Does trade cause growth?" *American Economic Review*, 89(3): 379-99.

Gramiccia, G., & Beales, P., (1988), "The recent history of malaria control and eradication," in Wersdorfer, W., & McGregor, I., eds. *Malaria: principles and practice of malariology*. New York: Churchill Livingstone.

Gwatkin, F., (1980), "Indications of change in developing country mortality trends: the end of an era?" *Population and development review*, 6(4): 615–44. .

Jamison, D; Sandbu, M; W, Jia, (2001), "Cross-Country Variation in Mortality Decline, 1962-1987: The Role of Country-Specific Technical Progress," *Commission on Macroeconomics and Health Working Paper Series*, World Health Organization #WG1:4.

Owen, A. L. and Wu, S. (2007), "Is trade good for your health?" *Review of International Economics*, 15(4): 660-682.

Oxfam (2007), "All costs, no benefits: how TRIPS-Plus intellectual property rules in the US-Jordan FTA affect access to medicines", available at http://www.oxfam.org/en/policy/bp102_jordan_us_fta

Popkin, B, and Du S. (2003), "Dynamics of the nutrition transition toward the animal foods sector in China and its implications: a worried perspective", *The Journal of Nutrition*, 133 (11): 3898S-3906S.

Raphael, (2004), "Social Determinants of Health: Canadian perspectives", Toronto, CSPI.

Rodriguez, F. and Rodrik, D., (1999), "Trade Policy and Economic Growth: A Skeptic's Guide to Cross-National Evidence", NBER Working Paper No. 7081.

Sachs, J. & Warner A., (1995), "Economic reform and the process of global integration", *Brookings Papers on Economic Activity*, (1):1–118.

San Sebastián, M. *et al.* (2006), "Is trade liberalization of services the best strategy to achieve health-related Millennium Development Goals in Latin America? A call for caution", *Pan American Journal of Public Health*, 20(5): 341-346.

Shaffer, E, & Brenner, J, (2004), "International Trade Agreements: Hazard to Health?" *International Journal of Health Services*, 34(3): 467–481.

Stevens, P. & Linfield, (2010), "Death and taxes: government mark-ups on the price of drugs", International Policy Network, London.

Wei. S-J., & Wu, Y., (2002), "The Life and Death implications of globalization", *IMF Working Paper* (Washington: International Monetary Fund).

World Health Organization, (2004), "World Medicines Situation", Geneva.

World Health Organization, (2008), "Final Report of the Commission on the Social Determinants of Health", Geneva.

World Health Organization (2011), "From burden to 'best-buys': Reducing the economic impact of non-communicable diseases in low and middle income countries", Geneva.

World Health Organization (2011), "Essential Medicines for Non-Communicable Diseases", Background paper, Geneva.

Yadav, P, (2010), "Differential Pricing for Pharmaceuticals", DFID: London.

2

THE HEALTH OF NATIONS: CONCEPTUALIZING APPROACHES TO TRADE IN HEALTH CARE

Fredrik Erixon[1]

"East is East and West is West, and never the twain shall meet." Are not the worlds of free trade and healthcare as much apart as the longitudinal extremes in Rudyard Kipling's famous ballad? Or, to put it differently: why are the forces of the wealth of nations not at work for the health of nations?

In the last fifty years, trade liberalization has progressed and spurred economic growth. Countries have liberalized, tariffs have been reduced, and other protectionist measures weakened. The structures and patterns of trade have also changed considerably. An increasing number of countries have integrated into the world economy. Multinational firms have fragmented their supply chains and used the opportunities created by trade and investment liberalization.

Yet there is one sector which remains conspicuously un-globalized and outside this trend of emerging free trade: health care. Health care has not completely escaped the forces of global integration, however. Input goods, like health technologies and pharmaceuticals, are traded. But the provision of healthcare services is not only essentially locked to international trade agreements in most developed countries, it also continues to be viewed as a non-tradable sector that, regardless of policy choices, cannot be traded.

This view is fundamentally misguided. Not only *can* healthcare be traded, it *is increasingly* traded. Yet there are several groups that continue to oppose trade in healthcare and attempt to block policy reforms that open the health sector for cross-border exchange. Some of these groups are entirely against trade and globalization; they, however, are largely street theatre on the fringes. More important and influential are established organizations and various United Nation bodies (including the World Health Organization), which either explicitly oppose any suggestion of freer trade in healthcare (without being critical of trade in other sectors) or that, under the flag of concern for developing nations, promulgate industrial policy models that trade in healthcare.

This chapter discusses current developments concerning trade in healthcare and related policy debates. The chapter aims to scrutinize various concepts of trade in healthcare and outline policy approaches. Its approach to trade in health is based on the age-old insights of the general benefits from trade, and it applies these benefits, framed in trade policy, to the world of healthcare.

The fiscal clamp on healthcare

The clearest trend in modern healthcare systems, particularly in advanced industrial economies, is rising expenditure. Estimates suggest that global expenditure in the early 21st century was as high as 3 trillion USD.[2] The OECD estimates that average health care expenditure in 2007 accounted for 9% of GDP, up from just over 5% in 1970.[3] Rising expenditures will continue in future decades as populations age, and governments will therefore need to contain costs without sacrificing service quality. Few have so far succeeded, and most healthcare systems are in a perpetual state of reform and flux.

The old model of increasing taxation to fund greater spending is no longer viable, as many countries have reached the limits of taxation without severely impinging on economic growth. New models of delivery and financing will have to be embraced if governments are to meet increasing demand for healthcare.

Technological development and new innovations place politicians and health administrators in a dilemma. They cannot provide public resources to pay for all new innovations and must find ways to restrict supply. Such methods, like health technology assessments and other cost-benefit analyses of new treatments are sometimes effective. Yet they can also be arbitrary and discriminatory. The basis for using some of the models of assessments is cost containment rather than an honest cost-benefit analysis which could provide an informed view to policy makers.

There is also another concern. Many of the methods used to control costs are focused on *new* costs; expenditures on *new* treatments, technologies, investments, and drugs. Put differently, cost-containing methods are often not focused on the major part of healthcare expenditure, which is constituted by the annual current spending on hospitals, salaries, infrastructure, etc. In fact, the organization of healthcare delivery is a strong denomi-nator not only of costs in general, but also of increasing costs. In many countries productivity is negative, despite increasing investments to substitute labour or in other ways increase more efficient use of resources. Healthcare inflation is far above standard consumer price indexes or home market-based price indexes.

Healthcare and trade policy

The potential for trade in healthcare and related goods and serv-ices is far from exploited. In fact, current trade in healthcare is a marginal phenomenon and there is no real systematic related trade policy.

As the locus of multinational trade liberalization, the World Trade Organization (WTO) has largely failed to produce results in terms of sub-stantial advancements of healthcare or by prompting liber-alization of domestic services around the world.

There are some WTO agreements that are relevant to health. In the agreements of Technical Barriers to Trade (TBT), Sanitary and Phytosanitary Measures (SPS), and Trade-related Intellectual Property Rights (TRIPS), there are direct linkages to trade in health-related products, but they do not cover trade in healthcare provision.

Box 1. The GATS structure

Trade in Services (GATS)

The health sector is covered under the following main sub-sectors:

1. BUSINESS SERVICES

a. Professional services

b. Medical and dental services

c. Veterinary services

d. Services provided by midwives, nurses, physiotherapists and paramedical personnel.

8. HEALTH RELATED AND SOCIALSERVICES

a. Hospital services

b. Other human health services (ambulance; residential health facilities)

c. Social services.

The General Agreement on Trade in Service (GATS), in which healthcare service trade is differentiated by four modes of supply, is most relevant to health service delivery and trade. As Box 1 and Table 1 show, there are areas in the GATS which relate directly to trade in healthcare services. However, WTO member countries have not agreed to any substantial liberalization in these areas. In fact, GATS has arguably achieved the least to date in terms of facilitating health-related cross-border exchange. Most information to date suggests that patterns and levels of trade in health services are occurring irrespective of GATS. This is most likely attributable to national commitments that bind existing levels of market access, rather than involving any substantial liberalization.

Table 1: Categorizing trade in healthcare in the language of GATS

Mode of Supply	*Specific Health Services*
Mode 1: Cross-border services trade	◆ Telemedicine – telediagnosis, surveillance and consultation services ◆ Electronic care delivery ◆ Medical education and training ◆ E-health (products and services available over the internet)
Mode 2: Consumption abroad	◆ Movement of patients seeking treatment abroad ◆ Movement of medical students and health profes-sionals studying and training abroad
Mode 3: Commercial presence	◆ Foreign direct investment, cross-border mergers or joint ventures for: ◆ Establishment of hospitals, clinics, nursing homes ◆ Management and insurance
Mode 4: Movement of natural persons	◆ Skilled health personnel, i.e. e doctors, nurses, paramedics, midwives, consultants, trainers, management

There are very few countries that have committed themselves to full liberalization in the health and social services sector under the prevailing GATS regime. Table 2 shows the small number of those that have, under modes 1 – 3.

Table 2: Full Commitment to Health Service Liberalization under GATS

Medical and dental services	Brunei, Burundi, Congo, Gambia, Guinea, Hungary, Iceland, Malawi, Norway, Rwanda, South Africa, Zambia
Midwives, nurses etc.	Gambia, Malawi, Norway, Zambia
Hospital services	Burundi, Ecuador, Gambia, Hungary, Jamaica, Malawi, Saint Lucia, Sierra Leone, Zambia
Other human health	Burundi, Gambia, Hungary, Malawi, Sierra Leone, Zambia
Social services	Gambia, Hungary, Sierra Leone

What is immediately obvious looking over the countries listed in table 2 is that the majority of WTO members with full commitments across modes 1 - 3 are developing countries. This is highly surprising if one considers the fact that part of the critique of liberalizing trade in healthcare, especially from Europe-based NGOs, claims devel-oping countries to be adversely affected by demands from richer countries to open healthcare and other public sector markets in the developing world. However, apart from Iceland and Norway, no developed country has committed to full liberalization.

There are some explanations for this trend, the first being that governments of developing countries are using GATS to lock in stable market conditions with a view to attracting foreign health providers. The second explanation, though, is that strong commitments are found in the health sector because they have found it politically easier to commit in an area where large-scale inflows are un-likely to occur, given the absence of attractive commercial opportunities. By doing so, fewer commitments in other, more sensitive areas are easier to justify. Of the sub-sectors that have been committed under GATS, it is also clear that members are more prone to full commitment in medical, dental and hospital services over and above services provided by midwives, nurses etc. This would suggest that governments are less keen to liberalize the labour-intensive activities within their health services, probably due to the current provision of government services at little or no cost.

A third explanation suggests that developing countries especially have fewer vested domestic interests lobbying against opening the healthcare sector for trade.

The lukewarm reception of the liberalization opportunity presented by GATS also (to a large extent) reflects the historically ingrained regulatory restrictions and institutional constraints that exist in domestic healthcare sectors, reflecting traditional views of healthcare and preventing cross-border movement of services. Such constraints are problematic from a trade perspective because, at the domestic level, health services are influenced by measures not normally considered to be "trade measures." There are three types of regulation employed by states that are most relevant to services trade in terms of affecting the supply or demand of health services:

1. Qualification and licensing requirements for health professionals.
2. Approval requirements for institutional suppliers, e.g. the range of goods and services that hospitals are allowed to provide.
3. Rules governing reimbursement and insurance schemes, e.g. a regulated domestic insurer may be prevented from reimbursing the cost of treatment abroad.

Others include the direct provision of services to economically disadvantaged groups and controls designed to ensure the adequate spread of services geographically within a state. All these measures are related to quality control and equity of access. There is considerable disagreement as to whether such measures should be subjected to the scrutiny of multilateral trade considerations. While some see them as trade restricting and discriminatory, others view them as vital instruments of national social policy. As a result, multilateral negotiations have been hampered by the difficultly of designing international rules that distinguish protectionist from legitimate policies. A purely economic analysis would view much existing healthcare regulation as another form of industrial policy with all its associated adverse economic implications, but many health administrators are critical of any analysis that emphasizes trade and commercial policy objectives, to the alleged detriment of equity and social policy considerations.

Trade policy for healthcare goods

The potential for trade in healthcare related goods has been better exploited than trade in healthcare services. Input trade is very advanced and subject to standard trade agreements for goods. Thus, equipment used in healthcare is often traded under a fairly ambitious trade agreement.

Table 3 shows current applied tariff levels on health products for a selection of WTO members. Not all countries, seemingly, are supportive of trade agreements which reduce tariffs to zero or close to zero. The persistence of tariff peaks in certain countries and for certain products reveals a similar propensity to domestic protection of healthcare industries in those countries that have significant industries. Brazil, India and Thailand stand out, but they are by no means alone. Even the US and Malaysia, which claim an effective tariff rate of zero overall, still introduce quotas if imports exceed specific volumes or weights. These countries are effectively employing industrial policy strategies, and the trend over the past two decades has been rising levels of protection.

Brazil, India, and Thailand are interesting examples. They are, on the one hand, part of the rising trend of "healthcare tourism". They have export strategies focused on attracting patients from other countries. On the other hand, they operate under fairly high tariffs for medicaments and health-related products. Furthermore, they have all had a propensity to infringe on other countries' intellectual property in the field of medicines.

Table 3: Healthcare related tariffs for Selected WTO Members

Country/ Trading entity	*Tariff*	*Biological products for Therapeutical Users*	*Medica-ments products**	*Health related products**	*Healthcare related apparatus and instruments*
	Lowest	2.56	3.71	2.88	4.75
Brazil	Average	4.20	9.74	10.27	8.74
	Highest	6.29	14.00	12.73	12.75
	Lowest	3.00	5.29	4.68	4.41
Chinese	Average	3.00	5.36	4.68	4.66
	Highest	3.00	5.57	4.68	4.94
European	Lowest	0.00	0.00	1.18	0.25
communities	Average	0.00	0.00	1.25	0.25
	Highest	0.00	0.00	1.79	0.25
	Lowest	30.00	30.00	21.82	25.63
India	Average	30.00	30.00	21.82	23.63
	Highest	30.00	30.00	21.82	23.63
	Lowest	0.00	0.00	0.00	0.00
United	Average	0.00	0.00	0.23	0.05
States**	Highest	0.00	0.00	0.45	0.19
	Lowest	0.00	0.00	1.82	0.00
Botswana	Average	0.00	0.00	2.73	0.55
	Highest	0.00	0.00	3.64	1.09
	Lowest	2.71	2.36	4.36	2.13
Philippines	Average	2.71	2.69	4.36	2.13
	Highest	2.71	2.71	4.36	2.13
	Lowest	0.00	8.00	1.32	5.50
Korea	Average	0.00	8.00	1.58	5.50
	Highest	1.14	8.00	2.05	5.50
	Lowest	0.00	0.00	1.67	0.00
Malasia	Average	0.00	0.00	1.67	0.00
	Highest	0.00	0.00	1.67	0.00
	Lowest	0.43	10.00	10.45	1.13
Thailand	Average	0.57	10.00	10.91	1.13
	Highest	0.71	10.00	11.36	1.13

All this might sound appealing to a proponent of infant-industry protection: a country, such as Brazil, uses protective instruments in order to build up its own industries, which later can become exporters. However, such policies have been highly ineffective in other areas and certainly have adverse effects in the fields of healthcare too. Leaving aside the specific issues of infringing on protected intellectual property - which is hardly a sustainable strategy for building up export champions - input tariffs raise the price of export. The old Lerner symmetry theorem (an import tax works as an export tax) is valid in general, but particularly so in sectors where import is necessary in order to export. In a country that wishes to export healthcare, input tariffs increase the price of its export. For developing countries, it is crucial to reduce barriers to import if they want to develop export strategies, especially if customers targeted are in developed countries and require high-quality healthcare. The same conclusion also applies to pharmaceuticals, and a serious drawback for countries like India and Thailand has been external suspicion over the quality of medicines coming from the domestic generic industry.

Opposition to liberalizing trade in healthcare

Despite the lack of any meaningful liberalization of healthcare services prompted by the WTO, the fact that healthcare is included in trade negotiations has provoked opposition from a range of actors. Arguments tend to be based on the "fundamental human right" of populations to healthcare and the perceived inherent difference of interest between profit-making businesses and those of society at large. This leads firstly to the assumption that the inclusion of healthcare services in trade agreements, especially WTO agreements, is a reflection of the spread of globalization, motivated by profit, and is threatening to outpace the ability of national governments to provide for their populations. Secondly, as the responsibility for healthcare delivery must therefore remain in the public sphere, healthcare services are by nature non-tradable.

Concerns have been expressed particularly over the effects on developing countries' healthcare systems if trade is increased. For example, John Hilary of Save the Children writes: "The specific provisions of GATS undermine the ability of countries to implement their own public health priorities ... governments must ensure that public health concerns are guaranteed absolute precedence over the economic aspects of services trade, in order to fulfill their responsibilities to ... society as a whole."[4]

But they are not confined to developing countries. Public sector unions in several developed countries have campaigned heavily against the GATS, especially before and in the first years of the Doha Round. The current practice of cross-subsidization within the healthcare sector is one issue that is being jealously guarded by influential bodies, such as the Royal College of Nursing in the UK. They are concerned that GATS will stop this practice altogether, as non profit-making services will be pushed out of the market.[5]

As a result of such lobbying, governments, especially in Europe, opted for huge carve outs in the healthcare sector in their commitment schedules when the GATS was negotiated in the Uruguay Round. This pressure was even evident in typically free-trade minded Sweden, which also, surprisingly, made the fewest commitments in the group of EU-15 members in its initial GATS offer in the Doha Round.

Trade in healthcare also seems akin to a foreign language when looking at current international discussions about healthcare delivery and priorities for co-operation between states. There are several United Nations (UN) bodies which operate in the field of healthcare, and evidence of caution, if not hostility, to increasing trade can be found amongst them. The World Health Organization (WHO), the leading UN body in the field of health, is one of them. It is not always easy to define the WHO's policy position. This is not surprising as it is a member-driven organization which operates mostly on the basis of unanimity. The WHO does not have an official view on trade in healthcare, and it rarely happens that the WHO promulgates views on health policy choices, since it requires endorsement of all member states. Yet policy analysis and policy formulation is a key activity of the WHO secretariat, and the secretariat largely works in a political discourse with a distinct ideological bent. Its work on trade and trade policy is no exception.

Conceptualizing approaches to trade in healthcare

The WHO discourse serves as a useful tool for comparison, when conceptualizing an exchange-oriented model for healthcare. Table 4 categorizes different features in the WHO approach to trade in healthcare and compares it with the view of a WTO discourse. The WTO is also a member-driven organization and does not have a specific programme that it campaigns for. Yet the WTO, as the WHO, operates in a discourse, constituted by international economics and international commercial law, with an ideological bent in favour of freer trade, the centrality of trade rules, and non-discrimination principles. The table is not an attempt to give an exhaustive presentation of all relevant viewpoints, but to distil the key and prioritized notions in a number of conceptual categories. Naturally, the WHO discourse leans more towards healthcare and the WTO approach towards trade.

Table 4: Conceptualizing approaches to trade in healthcare

Topic	*WHO discourse*	*WTO discourse*
Approach to cross-border exchange and integration	Critical approach to the phenomenon of trade when developing countries are involved. The North-South nexus is a dominant paradigm in most of its views. Health is defined as a human right, and thus the delivery of healthcare is a human obligation. Critical of market-based solutions.	Market-based approach. Trade is not only a natural phenomenon in markets; it is the key feature of markets.
Determinants of exchange	Trade in healthcare and health-related products is a one-way relation that mostly benefits exporters in developed countries. Favours a more planned model of trade, rather than a model based on specialization and comparative advantage.	The economics of specialization and scale; comparative advantage. Market-based structure of trade, in which demand and supply determines what and with whom to trade.
Aim of trade liberalization	Trade might have good outcomes. Yet the entire structure of motivation for trade rests on its contribution to greater equity. If trade is not equitable – and equitable seems in WHO language to mean distributive equality – it does not have a justifiable aim.	Trade liberalization can be motivated by different reasons. It has winners and losers, but in the medium-and-long term perspective it encourages more efficient use of resources, creates better opportunities to increase welfare and offers a vehicle for growth, in developed as well as developing countries. However, it is impossible to give assurances of the distributional outcomes of

Table contd...

Topic	*WHO discourse*	*WTO discourse*
		trade, especially assurances of greater equity, as liberalization spurs dynamic processes.
Intellectual property rights	Overhaul the system of intellectual property rights, at least as far as pharmaceutical patents are concerned. Greater flexibilities in TRIPS, such as the use of compulsory licensing for developing countries, especially for least developed countries without own production capacity. Develop other models of reward, such as prizes. Discourage TRIPS-plus provisions in bilateral trade agreements.	Favours multilateral agreements on trade-related issues concerning IPRs. TRIPS is a balance between the long-term objective of providing incentives for future inno-vation and creations, and the short-term objective of allowing people to use existing inventions. TRIPS establishes a basic level of protection, which needs to be safeguarded.
Industrial policy ambitions	Strong industrial-policy bent and a contingency-planning outlook. Build up domestic structure in healthcare delivery: hospitals, healthcare centres, etc rather than considering future trade opportunities Aid-induced exchange from developed countries to developing countries. Domestic build-up of research and innovation capacity in developing countries, especially in the pharmaceutical sector. Larger share of GDP and revenues in developing countries should be distributed to R&D and innovation with the view to build their own capacity.	Avoid situations when industrial policies distort trade or act as barriers to trade. Some flexibility - such as policy space - might be called for on certain occasions, but they are largely ineffective and discourage trade and economic growth.
Trade agreements	Cautious approach. Appropriate information vital about effects of trade agreements, especially in the fields of services, SPS, and IPRs. Only potentially negative aspects of trade agreements are presen-ted, also in areas where developing countries have made the highest number of commitments.	Multilateral trade agreements preferable to discriminatory agree-ments, but their existence and political realities are and political realities are recognized.
Movement of natural persons	Movement of health professionals from developing countries to developed countries is negative. Retention schemes promoted.	Viewed as a natural part of trade, especially in services. Labour migration encouraged, as such factor movements are beneficial.

Table contd...

Topic	*WHO discourse*	*WTO discourse*
Sources of protection	Protection is a natural state of affairs in healthcare. It is a consequence of other and more important political choices. For developing countries protection is often a necessity. Tariffs on health technology, though, should be abolished.	Government structures of regulations (tariffs, border protection, non-tariff barriers, and regulations). Protection is essentially a home-grown pheno-menon, and it typically favours a particular group at the expense of general welfare.
Governance structure	Global coordination of all issues related to health and healthcare. Multi-stakeholder approach involving many parties (governments, NGOs, private firms, et cetera) in common global strategies. Strong bent in favour of NGO participation as part of "global democracy;" NGOs participate in all decision-making forums in the WHO.	More co-operations with other international organizations and with the NGO community. Rests on a structure of governmental participation and a tradition of strong business participation.
Government planning	The source of health deve-lopments. Ten-year plans and very concrete action plans are favoured.	Market-based orders rather than government planning.

Each section of this table could be elaborated upon at greater length, but it is fairly obvious that these two discourses are fundamentally different. They have different origins, sets of ambitions, and understandings of policy. They represent different constituencies and come from different policy traditions. But will they, as in Kipling's ballad, never meet?

They probably *will* meet. If, for no other reason than the potential benefits of increasing trade-based integration of healthcare are too great not to be exploited. Three aspects deserve greater attention in this context.

1. The WHO discourse stresses healthcare as a fundamental human right. Traditionally it has favoured a governments-only approach to the delivery of healthcare – the means by which this particular right can be served. But there is an increasing awareness in the WHO community that

governments in many ways do not have a monopoly on the design of good healthcare systems.

2. Increased trade in healthcare is not a distant hypothesis; it is a reality closing in on many health policy matters - from the design of health insurance policies to regulatory structure. The issue, therefore, is not whether trade will increase or not. It is fairly obvious it will. The key question is rather in which form liberalization of trade in healthcare should be addressed and regulated: in a multilateral or bilateral form? Even the WHO favours a multilateral approach.

3. There is not likely to be substantial liberalization of trade in healthcare emerging from trade agreements. Previous trade agreements (with the notable exception of some bilateral agreements) have hardly led to concrete liberalization of trade in healthcare. Not even the EU, which provides the strongest regional trade agreement on record, has provisions for such trade, let alone strong pro-visions for trade in services generally. Therefore, the speed of liberalization will be slow and the process will be incre-mental. In trade agreements, countries are likely to bind only what they already have done at home. Trade-related reforms of healthcare are thus likely to be domestic and not imposed from external organizations.

Mapping a positive approach to trade in healthcare

Healthcare policies cannot only be a function of trade policy. But trade does hold some very tangible potential benefits for this sector. Trade in health services has been boosted by recent de-velopments in the high-tech industry. Cross-border tele-medicine, care delivery, diagnosis and treatment, medical education and training, and technical expertise have become increasingly available through the adaptation of new telecommunication devices and lower transaction costs. For example, e-learning programmes have made high quality education more readily accessible.

Telemedicine remains the sector with the largest potential benefits to health policy objectives. Up to now, however, its development has been constrained by regulatory deficiencies. National regulators have not had the tools to address the issue of medical malpractice liability in cross-border trade, and national health systems have retained diverse and cumbersome professional certification regulations. Public and private health insurances have rarely offered reimbursement of medical costs incurred abroad. As a consequence, cross-border telemedicine (or healthcare) is not yet fully developed and is usually used in one-way exchanges rather than in a potentially more efficient two-way exchange.[6]

Developing countries in Asia in particular (but also elsewhere) have recently seized on the trade potential from health tourism. In the past two decades, countries like Thailand, Malaysia, Singapore and Cuba have been taking advantage of low production costs to specialize in the export of hospital, medical and dental services. As such, they are becoming a destination for people travelling expressly to receive healthcare. In 1995–1996, Cuba was already generating 25 million USD in health tourism revenues by attracting more than 25,000 for-eign patients.[7] Health tourism has also brought considerable returns to Malaysia, Singapore and Thailand and a significant upward trend in the number of patients in Thailand. Later figures suggest a rapid increase in health tourism. In 2006, for example, Singapore had more than half a million foreign patients.

Trade in healthcare also involves foreign investments, or, to use GATS language, commercial presence. There are two key positive externalities from commercial presence for the host economy. Firstly, inflows of capital represent resources previously unavailable domestically. These, if channeled appropriately, can free domestic resources to be invested in other sectors of the health system. Secondly, foreign investors may introduce managerial skills that can be passed on to national health providers. As such, the additional resources could be used to upgrade healthcare infrastructure, introduce new technology, generate employment and provide sophisticated capital-intensive medical services.

The opening of Chile's health service, for example, resulted in large investments in infrastructure and services. The high competition between private providers for scarce resources led them to provide differentiated and high quality services by means of importation of medical supplies and equipment. This improved not only the quality of health services provided to the population, but also the work environment and labour demand to operate the imported equipment. It generated employment and stemmed the external brain-drain in the health sector.[8]

Temporary migration also represents a channel of trade. At the international level, this has been one of the most contentious areas of services liberalization because of the association with immigration law. Most limitations on the movement of health personnel are, in GATS language, horizontal limitations, applying to all services sectors.[9] Developed and developing countries alike, however, need to consider the benefits that increased immigration could bring. Importing countries gain greater availability of health professionals, who are becoming increasingly scarce in industrialized countries, exporting countries can take advantage of these professionals' remittance and the gain in human capital accumulated abroad.[10]

There are many examples of temporary flows of migrants which have been driven by conscious strategies, with the intention of earning foreign exchange and developing co-operation between governments. The Philippines, an important exporter of health professionals to ASEAN, Ireland, Kuwait, Libya, Saudi Arabia, the United States and the United Kingdom has established the Philippine Overseas Employment Administration to promote migrant labour. Other Asian countries have also been facilitating migration of medical staff to other countries as a way of increasing export and revenues. India, for example, has a significant number of doctors and nurses working in the UK and the US. Estimates from 2007 suggest 60,000 doctors of Indian origin are already working in the UK, contributing 8.9 billion USD to the UK economy. Overall, of the doctors working for the National Health Service (NHS) in the UK and Northern Ireland, 30 percent are estimated to have obtained their medical training outside an EU country.[11] As there is a growing scarcity of health personnel in many developed countries, and as the old-age dependency ratio is rapidly moving upwards, developing countries are taking a greater interest in securing access to rich markets.

Conclusions

Trade in healthcare is a growing phenomenon. Great benefits can be made by opening health sectors to trade and investment integration, but very few countries have undertaken such reforms. Even fewer countries have agreed to bind these structures of openness in trade agreements. The current increase in trade in health services has therefore emerged largely outside trade policy frameworks.

Current trade agreements have only scant and weak provisions for trade in health care. Some bilateral or regional agreements have provided for some healthcare integration, but most of them neglect this area. In the WTO, healthcare is part of the GATS agreements, but few countries have made strong commitments. Only a dozen countries, primarily developing countries, have committed to full liberalization.

The international health community, here defined through the WHO discourse, takes a skeptical if not hostile view of increased trade integration when it concerns North-South relations. It defines, erroneously, trade as being largely in the interest of developed countries, which tend to be pitted against that of developing countries. Its policy is not blatantly protectionist, but it errs on the side of protectionism and favours a strong industrial policy approach. This is especially true in the field of input goods trade, such as in medicines, but it is also reflected in healthcare policies.

This view is contrasted not only by some schedules of liberalization in the current WTO agreement, but also by the development of export strategies for healthcare in several developing countries. Countries as diverse as Brazil, China, Cuba, India, and South Africa are already significant exporters of healthcare.

Notes

1. Director and co-founder, European Centre for Political Economy, Brussels.
2. Chanda (2002).
3. OECD (2007).
4. Hilary (2001), p 9.
5. EPHA (2003).
6. Janjaroen & Supakankunti (2000).
7. Chanda (2002).
8. Blouin et al, eds (2002).
9. Adlung & Carzaniga (2001).
10. Blouin et al, eds (2002).
11. Kumar & Simi (2007).

Bibliography

Adlung, R & A. Carzaniga (2001), "Health services under the General. Agreement on Trade Services." *Bulleting of the World Health Organization*, 79(4): 352-364.

Arunanondchai, J & Carsten Fink (2007), "Trade in health services in the ASEAN region." Washington, DC: The World Bank (World Bank Research Policy Paper 4147).

Blouin, C, Nick Drager & Richard Smith, eds (2002), *International trade in health services and the GATS: current issues and debates*. Washington, DC/ Geneva: The World Bank/World Health Organization.

Chanda, Rupa (2002), "Trade in health services." *Bulletin of the World Health Organization*, 80(2): 158-163.

Davis, Lucy and Fredrik Erixon (2008), "Sweden: from free trade to protectionism?". Brussels: Euro-pean Centre for International Political Economy (ECIPE Policy Brief No. 01/2008).

Donaldson, Cam, Craig Mitton, & Virginia Wiseman (2005), *Economics of healthcare financing: the visible hand*. 2nd edition. New York: Palgrave Macmillan.

EPHA (2003), "The problems with trade for health." Brussels: European Public Health Alliance, available at <www.epha.org/a/337?var_recherche=problems+with+trade+for+health>.

Erixon, Fredrik & Erik van der Marel, (2008), *Determinants of health expenditures in Europe*. Brussels: Euro-pean Centre for International Political Economy (ECIPE).

Gómes-Dantés, O, J. Frenk & C. Cruz (1997), "Commerce in health services in North America within the context of the North America Free Trade Agreement." *Pan-American Journal of Public Health*, 1(6): 460-465.

Hilary, John (2001), "The wrong model: GATS, liberalization and children's right to health." London: Save the Children.

Janjaroen W & S. Supakankunti (2000), "International trade in health services in the new millennium: the case of Thailand." Bangkok: Centre for Health Economics, available at <www.who.int/trade/en/THpart3chap8.pdf>.

Kumar, P & T.B. Simi (2007), "Barriers to movement of health professionals: a case study of India." Jaipur: CUTS Institute for Regulation & Competition.

Mattoo, A & Randeep Rathindran (2005), "Does health insurance impede trade in healthcare services?" Washington, DC: The World Bank (World Bank Policy Research Working Paper 3667).

WHO/WTO (2002), *WTO agreements and public health: a joint study by the WHO and the WTO secretariat*. Washington, DC/Geneva: World Trade Organization/World Health Organization, available at <www.wto.org/english/news_e/pres02_e/pr310_e.htm>.

WHO (April 2007), "Background document for the Intergovernmental working group on public health, innovation and intellectual property (IGWG) proc-ess." Geneva: WHO Regional Office for Europe.

WHO (July 2007), "Draft global strategy and plan of action in public health, innovation and intellectual property: report by the secretariat." Geneva: Intergov-ernmental Working Group on Public Health, Innova-tion and Intellectual Property, Second Session (A/PHI/IGWG/2/2).

WTO (1998), "Health and social services: back-ground note by the secretariat." Geneva: Council for Trade in Services (S/C/W/50).

3

Do International Trade Regimes Restrict Access to Technologies in Developing Countries? The Case of Medicines

Philip Stevens

Introduction - IPRs, health and international trade rules

There is strong evidence that appropriate protection of intellectual property rights (IPRs) can facilitate technology diffusion in middle and lower-income countries. This spread of knowledge and technology occurs through increased trade in goods and services, foreign direct investment, joint ventures, licensing, and cross border-movement of personnel (Maskus, 2004). Additionally, IPRs can promote knowledge diffusion, as the information available in patent claims is publically available, and therefore easily accessible by other potential inventors who can use that information to invent around the patent to make improvements and modifications.

Despite this evidence, IPRs remain controversial with campaigners and 'public interest' groups who claim that they actively prevent technology diffusion, especially in the poorest countries. These complaints are heard loudest on the topic of patented medicines, and since the 1990s there have been a number of emotive global campaigns calling for an end - or at least a significant dilution - to IPRs in middle and lower-income countries. A critique common to such campaigns is that patents place too much power in the hands of rights holders, who use their temporary market exclusivity to inflate prices beyond what is reasonably affordable by the poorest. Furthermore, rights holders stand accused of using bilateral trade negotiations to impose IP standards that go beyond those required by the WTO's TRIPS agreement, thereby serving to delay unreasonably generic competition.

Perhaps the biggest global controversy on this topic to date has been the cost of patented HIV medicines in Africa. The issue first arose in South Africa in 1998, where in the face of a rapidly escalating public health problem; multinational companies launched a legal challenge in an attempt to prevent the government from diluting its patent laws. This court case attracted vocal and emotive opposition from local health activists and NGOs, whose campaigning promoted the impression in developed countries that multinational companies were profiting from a developmental emergency in poor countries by exploiting their patents to overcharge the dying and the poor for medicines – even though the then health minister stated on the record that even though ARVs were available at marginal cost, the state did not have the infrastructure or resources to provide continuous care for AIDS patients.[1] When the WTO met in November 2001, this local dispute was fresh in the minds of negotiators, and allowed for some concessions to be wrought from developed countries such as the US as the TRIPs agreement was renegotiated.

A concrete result of the 2001 meeting was the 'Doha Declaration', which inserted a number of flexibilities into the TRIPs agreement. Doha was widely presented as a success for developing countries, in large part because of the declaration on the TRIPs agreement and public health.[2] This declaration recognised the gravity of the public health problems affecting developing countries and affirmed the rights of these countries to "promote access to medicines for all" (paragraph 4), by granting compulsory licenses for health emergencies, and also giving member states the power to determine what constitutes a health emergency.

Activists lobbying for cheaper medicines before and during the Doha meeting hailed the Declaration as a victory for the developing world and an advance in their ability to address health crises, as it gave them freer scope to issue compulsory licenses and manufacture generic copies of patented medicines.

Since the Declaration and subsequent amendments, TRIPs flexibilities have indeed been invoked a handful of times, most notably by the military junta of Thailand in 2007 and by the government of Brazil in 2007. Paragraph 6 was invoked by Rwanda in 2007 to import generic ARVs from Canada, although this has had limited success (Attaran, 2010). In 2012, India also began to experiment with compulsory licenses for medicines.

IPRs in context

Despite all the political and diplomatic attention on the subject of international intellectual property of medicines, is it true that IPRs can actively discourage technology transfer in developing countries? In the case of patented AIDS medicines, it seems improbable. A 2001 survey by Amir Attaran and Lee Gillespie-White found that patents for ARVs are only occasionally registered in African countries, suggesting there are other factors at play that determine rates of access to these technologies, such as a lack of infrastructure, poverty and a lack of funding for healthcare generally.

A 2004 study by Amir Attaran found that 98 per cent of drugs on the World Health Organization's Essential Medicines List are off-patent. Many of the biggest killers of children in low-income countries - diarrhoea and respiratory infections - are easily preventable or treatable with cheap, off-patent medicines.

Even for non-communicable diseases, a growing problem in countries such as India, the majority of appropriate treatments are generic and available at a very low price (Table 1).

Table 1: Procurement Prices of Common NCD Medicines with no duties, taxes or mark-ups

Product	*Units /month*	*Median unit cost*	*Cost / month*
Glibenclamide 5mg tablet	30	$0.0034	$0.102
Metformin 500mg table	60	$0.0105	$0.63
Insulin NPH 100 IU/ml 10ml vial	1	$4.20	$4.20
Salbutamol 100µg/puff, 200 doses, HFA inhaler	1	$1.08	$1.08
Beclometasone 100µg/puff, 200 doses, HFA inhaler	1	$1.28	$1.28
Aspirin (ASA) 100mg tablet	30	$0.0019	$0.057
Simvastatin 20mg table	30	$0.0286	$0.858
Hydrochlorothiazide 25mg table	30	$0.0037	$0.111
Atenolol 50mg table	30	$0.095	$0.285

Source: NCD Alliance[3]

Despite these factors, an estimated 30 per cent of the world population lacks regular access to existing drugs, with this figure rising to over 50 per cent in the poorest parts of Africa and Asia (Figure 1). The evidence therefore suggests a poor *prima facie* case that patents *per se* block access to thousands of useful therapies, with other factors relating to the supply chain and infrastructure more likely culpable.

Figure 1: Percentage of WHO regions lacking Acess to Essential Medicines[29]

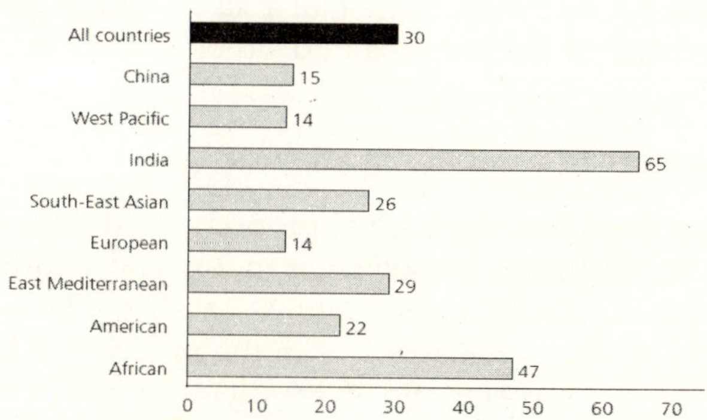

Source: World Health Organization

India provides a useful case study to determine the validity of the proposition that IPRs pose a barrier to access to technologies in developing countries, as for many years it afforded only very limited protection for intellectual property. In 1970, Indira Gandhi enacted legislation removing patent protection from pharmaceutical and agricultural products, proclaiming at the World Health Assembly in 1972, "The idea of a better ordered world is one in which medical discoveries will be free from patents and there will be no profiteering from life and death." But in spite of thirty years of patent-free drug production, access to even basic medicines in India remains unacceptably low. At the end of 2009 only a quarter of Indian HIV patients were receiving treatment.[4] This is in the face of the fact that 97 per cent of India's drug market consists of second and third generation drugs no longer subject to patent protection and is served by 6,000 licensed domestic generic manufacturers (Greene, 2007).[5]

In fact, the main consequence of the 1970 Act was to stifle product innovation and discourage foreign investment, while the Indian pharmaceutical industry developed a high volume / low value business model based on reverse engineering. To be sure, generic drug producers benefited, and India became one of the world's top five exporters of pharmaceuticals in volume, but the absence of product patents did not improve access to health technologies amongst the majority of the population. Meanwhile, the Indian software industry - protected by copyright - became of the most dynamic and innovative sectors of the Indian economy, growing from 1.2 to 5.8 per cent of GDP in 2009,[6] bringing with it many thousands of skilled jobs and other knock-on economic benefits.

The real barriers to access to medicines

It is clear, then, that intellectual property itself does not act as a barrier to the diffusion of medicines in low and middle-income countries. But as we have seen, access to all medicines - both patented and generic - remains low in the majority of lower and middle-income countries. So if intellectual property is not responsible for these low rates of access, what is?

The literature on technology diffusion in developing countries generally agrees that there are many other factors beyond IPR that determine rates of diffusion of technology, including: the absorptive capacities of local industries and businesses; physical infrastructure; restrictions on inward technology; trade and investment flows; and regulatory systems (Park and Lippoldt, 2008; Maskus, 2004). These factors can affect the demand for technology, by restricting the potential market size, and they can also undermine the supply of technology by making it difficult for companies to market and distribute their products.

These factors would seem to apply especially to medicines. Like many other forms of technology, medicines cannot simply be handed to consumers, but require a supporting infrastructure of clinics, professionals and appropriate regulation. Unfortunately, in many low and middle-income countries, weaknesses in these areas conspire to undermine access to medicines. The following section briefly outlines some of these weaknesses.

Lack of demand

In many low and middle-income countries, supply of health technologies is undermined by a lack of demand by patients. These barriers to demand can take many forms. The most obvious is poverty, as the majority of patients even in middle-income countries have to pay for care out of their own pockets, as a result of insufficient public or private health insurance coverage. In such circumstances, even the cheapest of generic medicines can be out of reach, let alone more expensive modern treatments requiring advanced diagnostics and high-tech delivery systems. Other demand barriers include the costs of healthcare uptake, such as travelling to clinics and foregone wages whilst treatment is being sought. Furthermore, many sick people do not have sufficient education to know about the availability or utility of healthcare (Ensor & Cooper, 2004).

Insufficient clinical infrastructure

In her acceptance speech at the World Health Organization in 2006, Director General Margaret Chan stated: "Health systems are the taproot for better health. All the donated drugs in the world won't do any good without an infrastructure for their delivery." This is certainly true - if healthcare systems are starved of resources and improperly managed, it is unlikely that they will be able either to procure and store necessary drugs or be able to employ sufficient numbers of doctors and other trained personnel necessary to prescribe and administer them.

Unfortunately, this is the situation faced by many countries. A particularly pressing problem is a shortage of qualified medical personnel in lower income countries (Table 2), a problem exacerbated by the 'brain drain' and exodus of locally trained doctors to wealthy countries such as the United States (Hagopian & Thompson, 2004). Meanwhile, patients have to contend with insufficient and dilapidated clinics and hospitals, fragmented supply chains, and shortages of diagnostic capacity. In many cases these infrastructural shortcomings can result in stock-outs in pharmacies (Pasquet et al, 2010),[7] leaving patients unable to access treatments at all.

Table 2: Global Health Workforce

WHO Region	*Number of health workers*	*Density/1000 population*
Africa	1640000	2.3
Eastern Mediterranean	2100000	4
South-East Asia	7040000	4.3
Western Pacific	10070000	5.8
Europe	16630000	18.9
Americas	21740000	24.8
World	59220000	9.3

Source: WHO, Global Atlas of the Health Workforce

Insufficient physical infrastructure

The problem of insufficient infrastructure is not limited to the clinical. The majority of low-income countries also lack the basic infrastructure required to distribute medicine successfully. Road networks are often unreliable or non-existent, making it difficult to ensure a constant supply of medicines to remote areas, and also for patients to visit clinics and pharmacies where medicines are dispensed (Brenneman, 2002). Electricity is often unavailable, especially in rural areas; where it is available, it is often supplied in an erratic fashion. This increases the cost and difficulty of running refrigeration systems in clinics and hospitals. As a result, products such as vaccines cannot be maintained at sufficiently low temperatures to ensure product stability.

Weaknesses in the supply chain

While drug distribution systems are typically reasonably effective at covering urban areas (where demand tends to be higher and infrastructure better) many rural areas often suffer shortages of supplies of even basic medicines. According to a study by the RAND Corporation these supply chain weaknesses fall into the following categories:

- Lack of standardized information systems
- Inefficient inventory accounting and management practices
- Lack of trained supply chain managers
- Limited tracking and tracing mechanisms
- Poor storage facilities and conditions
- Stock theft

These factors drive up costs, as well as making it more difficult to balance supply and demand for products.

Corruption

Supply chain weaknesses also increase opportunities for corruption, such as the insertion of counterfeit or substandard products into the supply chain, or theft. But corruption in healthcare is by no means limited to the pharmaceutical supply chain. It can occur at many levels, including direct embezzlement by ministers and senior officials; fraud in billing; local medical staff selling "free" drugs on the grey market, institutionalized absenteeism, and illegal payments to health care personnel that allow patients to jump queues or obtain treatment (Lewis, 2006; Transparency International, 2006). All of these instances of corruption reduce the amount of funding available for frontline delivery of medicines, and in many cases disrupt the supply chain, removing access to medicines altogether.

Taxes and tariffs

IPR is accused of limiting access to technologies by allowing manufacturers to exploit their market exclusivity and inflate their prices. While this may be theoretically true of patented medicines, many governments (especially in middle and lower- income countries) are guilty of inflating the price of both patented and generic medicines by adding a range of tariffs and taxes on imported and locally produced medicines. Nigeria, for instance, imposes a tariff of nearly 15 per cent on imported medicines, despite having amongst the worst health indicators in the world. The vast majority of high-income countries have abandoned tariffs on imported medicines on the grounds that they are regressive taxes on the poor and sick, but tariffs remain common in both lower and middle-income countries (Table 3).

In addition to tariffs on imported pharmaceutical products, many governments also levy a range of other taxes and mark-ups on medicines. Value added tax (VAT) is extremely common, as are sales taxes. Other duties include solidarity taxes, port charges and income taxes on local manufacturers. All these levies inflate the cost of medicines, making them less accessible for people who pay out-of-pocket.

Table 3: Tariff of pharmaceutical products in select countries

Country	*Tariff Rate (%)*
Argentina	9.10
Brazil	9.03
China	4.00
Egypt	2.58
Ghana	6.50
India	10.00
Indonesia	4.41
Israel	5.80
Mexico	6.88
Moroco	7.73
Nigeria	14.81
Pakistan	11.00
Russia	9.87
South Africa	0.00
Tanzania	0.00
Thailand	9.57
Turkey	0.00
Zimbabwe	8.00

Source: Stevens & Linfield, 2010

Non tariff barriers

In addition to visible tariff barriers, exporters and importers of medicines face numerous bureaucratic hurdles to the dissemination of their products. Exporters to China, for instance, cannot send their medicines to the most economically sensible port, but are restricted to one of eighteen ports designated by the government. For products that are being imported for the first time to China, there are only three designated ports. Other non-tariff barriers to trade in pharmaceuticals include complex language requirements on packaging, complex procurement procedures that favour local suppliers; lengthy and costly approval procedures by drug regulation and procurement bodies; burdensome import procedures that can add as much as 36 months to the process of bringing a product to market;[8] and lengthy and cumbersome registration procedures administered by local drug approval bodies.

The low purchasing power of the majority of citizens in poor countries means they do not constitute significant markets for foreign manufacturers. In the face of such non-tariff barriers, companies will often forego the regulatory complexity and expense of registering their products in that country and will instead invest their resources elsewhere. The result is that fewer medicines are approved — even when they are desperately needed - and there is a lower level of local competition in the marketplace which would otherwise drive prices down and increase access. In middle-income countries with a domestic pharmaceutical industry, non-tariff barriers act as a barrier to competition, resulting in higher prices for consumers.

Other barriers to access of technology

The foregoing provides some illustration of the kind of hurdles and barriers to the widespread distribution of medicines. For technology more generally, the World Bank has identified a number of other determinants of distribution, namely the extent to which a country has a technologically literate workforce and promotes and enables access to capital for high tech firms; the extent to which there is an investment climate that encourages foreign and domestic investment; and the existence of sufficient public sector institutions to promote the diffusion of technology in the absence of sufficient private demand. Other important factors in the dissemination of technology include a stable macroeconomic and political environment that can allow investment decisions to be made with some degree of confidence in the future, and the existence of diasporas who introduce foreign technologies and ideas to their home countries (World Bank, 2008).

What should be done?

This chapter has hopefully shown that in developing countries, IPRs rarely act as a barrier to access to medicines: the real culprits for low rates of access relate to broader issues surrounding the quality of infrastructure, regulation and governance.

Despite this complex landscape, many participants in global health debates continue to see the erosion of IPRs as a vital precondition for improving the health of citizens in developing countries, and advocate the outright abrogation of intellectual property rights via compulsory licenses (see, for instance, Bradford,

Kerry & Lee, 2007; Satyanarana, 2007; Mendis et al, 2007; and Cohen, Kohler & Lipkus, 2008). Such arguments revolve around the notion that patents act as a *de facto* barrier to access, and that flexibilities within the TRIPs agreement must be exploited so generic versions of patented drugs can be manufactured locally. Despite the large amount of advocacy that has taken place on behalf of this strategy, few compulsory licenses for have actually been fully implemented, with the exception of those in Thailand in 2006 and 2007, and Brazil in 2007. According to Ellen 't Hoen, senior advisor on intellectual property for UNITAID, "while most countries' national legislation contain provisions for use of compulsory licensing, it does not mean countries use it in practice."[9] Governments' reticence to use this policy measure may be partly to do with the risk to foreign direct investment that would result from compulsory licenses (Bird & Cahoynn, 2008), and that middle-income countries may use the threat of compulsory license as a bargaining chip in price negotiations with manufacturers (Bate & Boateng, 2007).

Voluntary licenses

Another mode of promoting generic competition and sidestepping onerous import regulations is via voluntary licenses. These allow (often local) generic companies to manufacture versions of patented medicines in return for a small royalty payable to the innovator. These licenses usually come with certain conditions and restrictions, for example limitations on export, helping to ensure that profits are not eroded by exports to high-income countries. In South Africa, foreign ARV rights-holders routinely license out their ARVs to local generic manufacturers, and the practice is becoming more widespread in India, which has significant generic manufacturing capacity. Licenses have also been issued to smaller African manufacturers. The majority of 2nd-line ARVs in use in sub-Saharan Africa are made by innovator companies, often in collaboration with local generics manufacturers via a voluntary license (Chien, 2007).

Although many voluntary licenses for manufacturing generic ARVs have been granted, they do not always result in drugs being manufactured and shipped to patients. It could be that the costs of scaling up production, marketing and distributing a product are too high for many generic manufacturers to turn a profit.

Although voluntary licenses have not yet shown themselves to be a 'silver bullet' solution, they are likely to have some utility as emerging markets become more wealthy and begin to register more demand for therapies for non-communicable diseases such as diabetes and cardiovascular and lung diseases. This extra demand will translate into greater economies of scale, making these voluntary licenses more viable. Voluntary licenses may therefore become a more realistic business proposition, which would allow cheap, high quality medicines to be widely distributed in lower-income countries.

Differential pricing

Voluntary licenses or unlicensed generic manufacture are two ways of increasing access to medicines. In the long term, however, these methods do little to support future research and development (R&D) as they typically only recover a fraction (if any) of the innovator's costs. Another method of increasing access while recouping those costs - and thereby incentivising future R&D - is for companies to sell a product at different prices to different consumers, depending on their ability to pay. In theory, so-called 'differential pricing' achieves the twin aim of increasing access for the poor while allowing the innovator to recoup the development costs from richer countries - plus the profit required to invest into future research and development.

Differential pricing and market segmentation has not been widely and systematically applied to medicines, although the situation for ARVs has changed considerably over the last decade. Prior to 2000, branded ARVs were similarly priced in both low and high-income countries (Hellerstein, 2004). Tiered pricing for ARVs was first introduced in 2000 with the creation of the Accelerated Access Initiative, when major pharmaceutical companies began to market their ARVs at two different tiers of pricing, with sub Saharan countries generally eligible for the discounted tier. Nowadays, the majority of pharmaceutical companies offer three tiers of price (high- income, middle-income and low-income countries), with the exceptions of GlaxoSmithKline (GSK), which offers a discounted price for sub-Saharan African countries; PEPFAR, and Global Fund financed projects. For every other country, GSK negotiates prices bilaterally or through the Accelerated Access Initiative (Yadav, 2010).

Despite the theoretical appeal of price differentiation, there are numerous hurdles to be overcome before it can become widespread and effective. One major barrier is the risk of physical arbitrage, wherein products earmarked for low-income markets get diverted to high-income markets, thereby simultaneously undermining revenues in high-income markets and reducing the supply in low-income markets. This risk was recognised by the European Union in May 2003, when it enacted regulation that prevented the re-importation of cheaper medicines sold to lower-income countries outside the EU. There is also the risk of governments of middle or high-income countries using the priced offered to lower-income markets as a reference price for their own public procurement. This would gradually lead to a unified global price, thereby undermining the welfare gains that would arise from market segmentation. Given the government exercises monopsony power over the market for pharmaceuticals in many countries, this risk is not unsubstantial.

Governments of middle-income countries have also complained that setting prices by the income of a country does not take account of income inequalities within countries: although India may be classed as a middle-income country, for instance, it has large numbers of citizens who are as poor if not poorer than the average citizen in a lower-income country like Burundi. This factor has been used by middle-income countries to push for ARV prices closer to those offered to low-income countries. Citing this factor, Brazil has repeatedly used the threat of compulsory licenses in ARV pricing negotiations to push for further price cuts, most notably in 2007 with Merck's ARV Efavirenz (Bate & Boateng, 2007).

As a result of the risks posed by physical arbitrage and external reference pricing, differential pricing has yet to be taken up widely by the pharmaceutical industry. However, there are indications that this strategy will become more widespread, especially given the increasing importance of emerging markets such as China and India. GSK, Merck, Novo Nordisk and Pfizer are all developing pricing strategies that allow them to sell certain patented products at lower-prices in developing countries. Emerging industry practice provides some hints at how some hurdles to widespread use of differential pricing may be overcome in the context of NCDs. One promising strategy is the use of market-specific branding and packaging. GSK has experimented with different packaging and pill colour for two of its ARVs marketed in developing countries (Combivir and Epivir) in order to reduce the risk of diversion back to wealthier markets, and as identity preservation and tracing technology develops (e.g. barcodes, RFID etc) such strategies will become more viable.

Conclusion

Access to medical technologies is the product of a complex interplay of factors including health financing, infrastructure, and regulation. At best, it is simplistic and reductive to blame low rates of access in lower and middle-income countries on IPRs. At worst, public campaigns that blame poor healthcare on IPRs remove pressure on governments to enact reforms to healthcare systems that would genuinely improve access to medicines. While such campaigns continue to emit more heat than light at the multilateral and domestic levels, policymakers would be wise to ignore such red herrings and focus on the genuine determinants of access to medicine: physical infrastructure, financing, medical personnel and supply chains.

Notes

1 The Citizen, Johannesburg, May 2000.

2. WTO (2001).

3. Available at http://ncdalliance.org/sites/default/files/resource_files/NCD%20Alliance%20briefing%20paper%20-

%20Access% 20to%20Essential%20Medicines% 20and%20 Technologies % 20for%20NCDs% 20(full%20references).pdf

4. UNGASS (2010, March 31st) 'India - Country Progress Report'.
5. Greene, W, (2007), "The Emergence of India's pharmaceutical industry and implications for the US generic drug market", US International Trade Commission.
6. NASSCOM as reported by India Brand Equity Foundation (2009), 'Information technology, Sector structure/Market size, 9 November: http://www.ibef.org/artdisplay.aspx?cat_id=114&art_id=24623
7. Pasquet A, Messou E, Gabillard D, Minga A, Depoulosky A, et al. (2010). Impact of Drug Stock-Outs on Death and Retention to Care among HIV-Infected Patients on Combination Antiretroviral Therapy in Abidjan, Côte d'Ivoire. PLoS ONE 5(10).
8. Federation of India Chambers of Commerce and Industry, "Non tariff barriers stump pharma exports to India", January 2007.
9. "Compulsory licensing of generic drugs remains mired in quagmires", Canadian Medical Association, June 24th, 2011.

Bibliography

Attaran, A. (2004), "How Do Patents And Economic Policies Affect Access To Essential Medicines In Developing Countries?" *Health Affairs*, 23(3): 155-166.

Attaran, Amir (2010), "Why Canada's Access to Medicines Regime Can Never Succeed." *UNB Law Journal*, 60: 150-160.

Bate, Roger and Boateng, Kathryn (2007), *Drug Pricing and Its Discontents: At Home and Abroad.* Health Policy Outlook paper no. 9. Washington, DC: American Enterprise Institute.

Bird, R and Cahoynn, D. (2008), "The Impact of Compulsory Licensing on Foreign Direct Investment: A Collective Bargaining Approach", *American Business Law Journal*, 45(2): 283–330.

Chami, Goldis and Wasswa-Kintu, Samuel (2011), "Compulsory licensing of generic drugs remains mired in quagmires" *Canadian Medical Association Journal*, 183(11).

Chien, Colleen V. (2007), "HIV/AIDS Drugs for Sub-Saharan Africa: How Do Brand and Generic Supply Compare?" *PLoSONE*, 2(3): e278.

Ensor, Tim and Cooper, Stephanies (2004), "Overcoming barriers to health service access: influencing the demand side." *Health Policy and Planning,* 19(2): 69-79.

FICCI (2007), "Non-tariff barriers stump pharma exports to India." *Federation of India Chambers of Commerce and Industry,* 27 Jan. http://www.ficci.com/press/230/press6.htm

Greene, William (2007), *The Emergence of India's pharmaceutical industry and implications for the US generic drug market.* Office of Economics Working Paper No. 2007-05-A. Washington, DC: US International Trade Commission.

Hagopian, Amy *et al.* (2004), "The Migration of Physicians from Sub-Saharan Africa to the United States of America: Measures of the African Brain Drain." *Human Resources for Health,* 2: 17.

Harris, Julian *et al.* (2009), *Keeping It Real: Combating the Spread of Fake Drugs in Poor Countries.* London: International Policy Network.

Hellerstein, Rebecca (2004), *Do Pharmaceutical Firms Price Discriminate Across Rich and Poor Countries? Evidence from Antiretroviral Drug Prices,* New York: Federal Reserve Bank of New York.

IBEF (2009), "Information technology: Sector Structure/Market Size", *India Brand Equity Foundation,* 9 November, available at, http://www.ibef.org/artdisplay.aspx?cat_id=114&art_id=24623

Love, James (2001), "Implementing TRIPS safeguards", *Consumer Project on Technology,* Aug 2001, available at http://www.cptech.org/ip/health/cl/harare-aug2001.html

Maskus, Keith E. (2004), *Encouraging International Technology Transfer,* UNCTAD-ICTSD Project on IPRs and Sustainable Development Issue Paper 4. Geneva: United Nation Conference on Trade and Development.

Park, Walter G. and Lippoldt, Douglas C. (2008), "Technology Transfer and the Economic Implications of the Strengthening of Intellectual Property Rights in Developing Countries." *OECD Trade Policy Working Papers* 62, Paris: Organisation for Economic Co-Operation and Development.

Pasquet, Armelle *et al.* (2010), "Impact of Drug Stock-Outs on Death and Retention to Care among HIV-Infected Patients on Combination Antiretroviral Therapy in Abidjan, Côte d'Ivoire", *PLoS ONE,* 5(10).

Plaza, Sonia and Ratha, Dilip (2011), "Harnessing Diaspora Resources for Africa" In *Diaspora for Development in Africa,* Edited by Sonia Plaza and Dilip Ratha. Washington, DC: World Bank. pp. 1-54.

Stevens, Philip and Linfield, Holly (2010), *Death and Taxes: Government Mark-Ups on the Price of Drugs.* London: International Policy Network.

Sunesen, Eva R. *et al.* (2010), "*Assessment of Barriers to Trade and Investment between the EU and Japan: Final Report*", Copenhagen: Copenhagen Economics. available at http://trade.ec.europa.eu/doclib/docs/2010/february/tradoc_145772.pdf

UNAIDS (2010), *Country Progress Report: India, 31 March 2010.* Geneva: Joint United Nations Programme on HIV/AIDS. available at http://www.unaids.org/fr/dataanalysis/monitoringcountryprogress/2010progressreportssubmittedbycountries/file,33667,fr..pdf

WTO (2001), *Declaration on the TRIPS agreement and public health, WT/MIN(01)/DEC/2.* Doha WTO Ministerial 2001, 20 November 2001, available at http://www.wto.org/english/thewto_e/minist_e/min01_e/mindecl_trips_e.htm

Yadav, Prashant (2010), *Differential Pricing for Pharmaceuticals: Review of Current Knowledge, New Findings and Ideas for Action.* London: Department for International Development.

4

Combating Trade in Counterfeit Drugs in Lower and Middle-Income Countries

Julian Morris[1]*, Julian Harris*[2] *& Philip Stevens*[3]

How big is the problem?

The global trade in fake medicines is vast and growing. It results in millions of people unwittingly consuming cement, talcum powder, sawdust, paint and an array of other toxic or inert substances. It thwarts efforts to cure disease and worsens illness. And perhaps worst of all, it results in the emergence of drug resistant strains of diseases ranging from AIDS and malaria to tuberculosis and bird flu (Miller, 2007; Stevens, 2006).

In wealthy countries, the discussion of fake medicines tends to focus on dangerous counterfeits imported into domestic markets (and state-run health services). While this problem seems to be worsening, the situation in poor countries – the focus of this paper – is already far more serious.

The paper is composed of four parts. The first looks at the scope of the problem in less developed countries (LDCs). The second examines the health impacts of fake medicines. The third section considers the main causes of the problem. The final section offers some possible solutions.

This chapter is about substances that are sold as medicines yet are not what they purport to be. Some of these substances are deliberately mislabelled, i.e. counterfeit. Others may have been inadvertently mislabelled or the pills contaminated during manufacture. Others may originally have been exactly as they claim, but due to poor storage have degraded and are consequently sub-standard.

It is sometimes argued that "counterfeit" drugs and "substandard" drugs must not be spoken of together, and the World Health Organization now has two separate definitions: counterfeits are "deliberately and fraudulently mislabelled" whereas substandard drugs are defined somewhat ambiguously as "genuine drug products" that do not meet pharmacopoeial standards.

In practice, overlaps between these two terms are inevitable. Studies in areas suffering from poor quality drugs typically discover counterfeit as well as substandard drugs, according to the definitions above. It can be extremely difficult to differentiate between the two, as it is not always clear whether or not the actions leading to faulty drugs were deliberate. Furthermore, the difference is of little concern to a patient harmed by bad medicine.

As it is difficult to distinguishing between counterfeit and substandard medicines, and because they both pose a considerable threat to health, for simplicity we will refer to all such medicines as "fakes".

The following statistics are often cited as demonstrations of the size of the global market:

- The World Health Organization (WHO) published estimates that counterfeit drugs constitute 10 per cent of the global drug market, rising to 25 per cent in LDCs
- A study by the Center for Medicines in the Public Interest predicted that global sales of counterfeit drugs were worth

$75 billion in 2010 (an increase of over 90 percent from 2005).

- The Pharmaceutical Security Institute estimates that seizures of counterfeit drugs in 2007 increased by 24 per cent on the previous year, with 1,513 seizures recorded in 99 different countries. These fakes were replicating over four hundred different types of drugs.[4]

Cumulative evidence suggests that there is a vast and growing global trade in fake drugs, yet more reliable statistics can be observed in the large number of investigations into levels of fake drugs in the worst hit parts of the world.

Worst affected regions

Fake medicines are most prevalent in poor countries. Estimates suggest that counterfeits represent up to a third of medicines in some LDCs – notably in Africa (Taylor, 2008). With non-counterfeit substandard medicines also highly prevalent in poor countries, the picture is bleak. The following studies in Sub Saharan Africa reinforce this finding:

- A study that sampled 22 ampicillin drugs on sale in Senegal discovered that 21 were made of flour. (Sow et al., 2002)
- 46 per cent of drugs in Angola, Burundi, and the Congo are substandard, another study estimates. (Gaudiano et al., 2007)
- A survey in Burkina Faso found that 10.6 per cent of drugs procured from licensed sellers were substandard, and 90 per cent purchased from unlicensed sellers were substandard. (Tipke at al., 2008)
- One study in Kenya revealed over 40 per cent of sampled drugs to be outside pharmacopoeial standards. (Amin et al., 2005)

The picture is similar in Asia. In 2006 a study throughout Laos, Myanmar (Burma), Vietnam, and Cambodia found that 68 per cent of artesunate (anti-malaria) drugs did not contain the correct amount of active ingredient (Alter Hall, 2006). The following year (2007) a team from Oxford University, Bangkok's Mahidol University and the Wellcome Trust conducted a survey in the same countries. Professor Nick Day of the research team is reported to have said: "In some areas 30–50 per cent, or even more than 50 per cent, of drugs you buy randomly from pharmacies are actually fake" (McGivering, 2007).

Sources of fake medicines

One set of figures from the European Commission showed 75 per cent of counterfeit drugs being imported from India[5], home to around 22,000 small drug producers, many of which are informal (Bate, 2008). The Associated Chambers of Commerce and Industry of India estimate this market is growing by 20–25 per cent per annum (Barnes, 2008; Bate, 2008; Lal, 2008).

A 2004 survey of medicines on sale at a large bazaar in New Delhi found that only 7.5 per cent were genuine. A report in an Indian newspaper said that fakes are freely sold to "exporters who sell them to unsuspecting health administrators in Sub-Saharan Africa, who receive some of the millions in aid money."[6]

After India, China is the second largest source.[7] Good data are hard to come by, yet anecdotal evidence suggests that fakes produced in China are prevalent both domestically and internationally. For example, in May 2008, six out of seven people injected with immunoglobulin in Jiangxi province died; subsequently, irregularities were found in samples of the drug (Juan, 2008).

A 2008 small sample study of anti-malarial drugs across Africa found that over 30 per cent of drugs originating in Asia failed quality checks. However, locally produced drugs fared even worse, with nearly half found to be substandard. (Bate et al., 2008).

Most faked medicines

In LDCs, fake medicines seem to be prevalent across all classes of drugs, as evidenced by the reports of counterfeit drugs received by WHO – see figure 1. Yet most cases of counterfeit drugs probably are not known to the governments of LDCs, since there is no systematic mechanism for discovering and disclosing them. Meanwhile, even those instances that are known to the authorities are not necessarily reported to the WHO – as evidenced by the fact that fewer than 5 per cent of the WHO's members have reported cases of counterfeiting (Bate, 2008).

Finally, counterfeits are only part of the problem, with other substandard items also being prevalent. The problem also extends beyond fake pharmaceuticals to medical consumables such as non-sterile syringes and gauze, and even substandard electronic medical equipment.

What are the dangers?

The main dangers to health posed by fake drugs are:

1. Failure to provide effective treatment
2. Direct harm
3. Drug resistance

A fake medicine typically causes at least one and often two or even all three of these effects, which we now discuss.

Failure to treat

The most common effect is the failure to provide successful treatment. This occurs when a fake contains insufficient quantity of the active ingredient, or I the delivery mechanism (the other ingredients that enable the drug to be taken up by the body) does not function properly. When a fake fails to treat a condition, the effect can vary from the relatively insignificant (such as when a fake analgesic does not alleviate a mild headache that subsides on its own) to the very serious (such as when a fake anti-malarial fails to destroy falciparum parasites and the patient dies).

Direct harm

In some cases, fakes cause direct harm to the patient. For example, paracetamol cough syrup contaminated with antifreeze (chemical names: ethan-1-2-diol or diethylene glycol) has killed hundreds of patients, including 339 children in Bangladesh in 1990, 85 children in Haiti in 1995, over 100 children in Panama in 2007. As of March 2009, more than 80 children are reported to have died in Nigeria after ingesting a teething mixture named "My Pikin". (Bogdanich and Hooker, 2007; Clark, 2008).

Drug resistance

Finally, when a fake drug, used to treat a disease caused by a virus, bacterium, parasite or other micro-organism contains some active ingredient, but not enough to eradicate the micro-organisms, the remaining micro-organisms breed, resulting in drug-resistant strains. As a result, the real medicine becomes less effective at treating the disease.

Resistance is currently a serious problem with tuberculosis, as stronger, deadlier mutations emerge such as the XDR-TB strain (Extremely Drug Resistant Tuberculosis), now confirmed in 49 countries ranging from Peru to Nepal (De Capua, 2008). According to the WHO, 5 per cent of new tuberculosis infections between 2003 and 2007 were multiple drug resistant cases, with the rate in some countries over 35 per cent (World Health Organization, 2008).

Widespread resistance is also a very serious problem with malaria. In the 1980s and 1990s anti-malarial drugs such as chloroquine and sulphadoxine / pyrimethamine were used inappropriately so that parasites became resistant to them. Those drugs were superseded by artemisinin, which is now used widely, usually in 'combination therapies' (ACTs) designed to prevent resistance. However, the success and effectiveness of ACTs is threatened by fakes, with evidence of resistance in the border areas of Cambodia, Laos, Vietnam and Myanmar (Burma), where fake medicines are highly prevalent (WHO, 2008). In the border town of Pailin, successful response to ACTs has declined from 85.7 per cent in 2002 to 79.3 per cent in 2004 (Wongsrichanalai, 2008).

Other consequences

Fakes also affect spending on research and development (R&D) into new medicines. Even near perfect copies of on-patent medicines cause harm by competing with legitimate supplies of medicines from originating companies, which reduces revenues and undermines incentives to invest in future R&D.

Furthermore, the production of substandard generic medicines can crowd out manufacturers of high quality generics, who have made costly investments in bringing their plants up to international Good Manufacturing Practice and bioequivalence testing.

If fakes are widespread, confidence in medicine is undermined, resulting in less demand and poor adherence to drug regimens (which in turn can provoke drug resistance).

What are the causes?

We now turn to analyzing the reasons for the prevalence of fake medicines in LDCs. A simplistic analysis might observe that there are more producers of fakes in poor countries, or claim that poor people are less willing to pay for quality medicines. While the first observation is true, it tells us little about why there are so many counterfeiters. Meanwhile, the claim that poor people are unwilling to pay for quality medicines implies that poor people are unable to make rational decisions; after all, why would someone pay for a medicine that they knew would do them no good?

We do not believe the poor are irrational. We believe that they are the victims of a combination of defective legal systems and government-imposed distortions of the pharmaceutical market.

Defective legal systems

Poor countries tend to be characterised by highly inefficient, bureaucratic, slow and expensive legal systems. In many such countries it is difficult formally to own property and to enter into contracts. We consider the implications of these and related issues in relation to the production, distribution and consumption of fake medicines.

Absent or defective trademark protection

One way to discourage the sale of unauthorised copies of medicines is to enable vendors to signal the quality of their product to potential purchasers. Trademark is one mechanism for doing that: brand owners have strong incentives to ensure that the quality of their product is maintained because their reputation and hence future profitability depend upon it. In many LDCs, it is difficult to enforce trademarks – even for local companies. Where trademarks cannot be enforced, cheaply produced poor quality copies will typically crowd out good quality drugs.

Lack of adequate civil liability

Civil law protects the consumer against mis-sold or defective goods. By enabling consumers (or their relatives) to obtain redress from the manufacturer or supplier of a harmful product, such liability both compensates those who are harmed and discourages manufacturers and suppliers from selling fakes. In many LDCs, however, civil law is either poorly defined or inadequately enforced.

This is reflected in the recent cases of fake ingredients in products ranging from pet food to baby milk manufactured by Chinese companies (melamine was added to products because it mimics protein in simple tests). While many Chinese victims have been unable to obtain redress from the perpetrators, American groups have sought compensation from the suppliers of Chinese pet food containing deadly fake ingredients and reports suggest the settlement could be in the order of $32 million. In the future pet food suppliers in the US will likely take greater care to avoid selling fake ingredients. Meanwhile, the only recourse Chinese parents have over the death of their children caused by contaminated baby milk is to sue a US subsidiary of one of the Chinese companies that produced the milk – in a US court![8]

The Confederation of Indian Industry lists the "inadequacy of civil jurisprudence" as one of the main reasons behind counterfeiting in India. They describe civil law procedure as "lengthy and cumbersome", and note that brand owners therefore view intellectual property theft as inevitable in the Indian market.[9]

Inability to resolve disputes over property rights and contracts in independent courts

In many cases, underlying the lack of civil liability and weak IP protection are costly and inefficient legal systems. It can often take years for cases to be heard and cost more to bring a case than the value of any outcome. Under such circumstances, few cases will ever come to court and the nominal protection offered by civil liability is of little value.

Weak or absent rule of law

Many LDCs lack constitutional provisions protecting the rights of citizens. In such countries, political and legal decisions tend to be arbitrary and designed to benefit the elite. Meanwhile, law enforcement also tends to be corrupt (Schleifer and Vishny, 2003). As a result, regulation designed to combat counterfeiting is often ineffective. Criminal counterfeiting gangs may be able to pay corrupt law enforcement agents to turn a blind eye to their activities. If a case does make it to court, the gangs may be able to pay off the judge and thereby induce a favourable judgment.

Added layers of government can increase opportunities for corruption, which are already rife in the health sectors of LDCs. Workers in state-run hospitals and clinics routinely resell 'free' pharmaceuticals on the black market, sometimes replacing them with counterfeit products (Lewis, 2006).

Government-imposed distortions of the medicines market

Governments in LDCs compound the problem of fake medicines through various interventions into the pharmaceutical market, such as taxes, tariffs, licensing regimes and price controls. These interventions lead to additional layers of bureaucracy, which in LDCs with a weak rule of law are easily exploited by unscrupulous officials and criminals. They also often exacerbate the imbalance between supply of and demand for high quality medicines. These gaps in supply of genuine medicines are readily exploited by criminals.

Tariffs and other import restrictions

Many governments in low and middle-income countries impose tariffs on imported drugs, and sales taxes on both domestically produced and imported drugs (Table 1). Such tariffs have the effect of driving up the price of good quality imported medicines, undermining efforts by drug companies to sell at lower prices in low-income areas, and even deterring them from entering the market at all.

Table 1: Average import tariffs and sales tax on pharmaceuticals for a selection of countries

Country	*Weighted average tariff (%)*	*VAT/GST (%)*
Burundi	15.00	
Nigeria	14.81	
Tunisia	13.02	6.00
Guyana	11.60	16.00
Trinidad & Tobago	11.35	
Pakistan	10.56	15.00
Jamaica	10.54	17.00
India	10.00	4.00
Bangladesh	8.32	15.00
Vietnam	6.36	10.00
Chile	6.00	19.00
Peru	9.00	19.00
China	4.13	17.00
Malaysia	0.00	0.00
Brunei	0.00	-
New Zealand	0.00	12.50
Australia	0.00	10.00
Japan	0.00	5.00
USA	0.00	
Canada	0.00	

Source: Stevens & Linfield (2010)

By increasing the price differential between quality medicines and fakes, such barriers create opportunities for counterfeiters. The need to pay tariffs creates extra layers of slow-moving customs bureaucracy. In addition, importers of genuine products face numerous bureaucratic hurdles that can be exploited by criminals. These tariffs and regulations often result in customs officials soliciting bribes in order to decide which drugs are held up and which are fast-tracked - a situation which favours importers willing to behave illegally, such as those supplying counterfeits.

To make matters worse, importers of legitimate medicines suffer the double whammy of paying high tariffs and having their medicines stored inadequately in customs warehouses, leading them to degrade. This not only has the effect of increasing the number of substandard (and potentially resistance-inducing) drugs in the market, it also undermines confidence in reputable, branded drugs. According to Andy Macaleer, Director of Pharmaceutical Solutions at Acsis (a company working on pharmaceutical supply chains), "the leading reason for the return of prescription drugs is due to products sitting in the supply chain too long and expiring before they can be dispensed" (Macaleer, 2008; Stevens, 2008).

Numerous studies have been performed into the degradation of drugs in transit (Hogerzeil et al., 1991; Hogerzeil et al., 1992; Nazerali et al., 1996), and some report particularly poor conditions in customs. In their study on factors leading to drug resistance, Okeke et al. cite the conditions drugs are exposed to in "tropical ports while they await lengthy port clearance".

Price controls

Many governments impose price controls on medicines. Ostensibly, these are intended to reduce the cost to consumers, be they individuals or Ministries of Health. However, they also result in many unintended harmful consequences.

Such price controls have several adverse effects. Firstly, they discourage companies from registering products in certain markets. Most disturbingly, it is often the producers of the highest quality brands who withdraw from the market; because they tend to have a higher cost base and their margins will be most affected by the price controls. Meanwhile, producers of cheaper, lower quality medicines and outright counterfeits are favoured.

Secondly, price controls encourage manufacturers to alter the nature of their products, in order to circumvent the controls. This problem is perhaps most acute in India, where there has been a surge in so-called 'irrational fixed dose combinations' - combinations of two or more drugs that have no clinical justification. Such combinations result in the consumption of unnecessary drugs, since patients often take the drug primarily for only one of its components. In addition, such combinations have rarely undergone clinical trials, so present unknown dangers to patients. As Urmila Thatte of BYL Nair Hospital and Research Centre in Mumbai points out, "The drugs may interact with each other, or may interact with food. They may even cause adverse reactions and a physician may find it impossible to identify which drug has caused it".[10] 60 per cent of the top-selling 300 drugs in India are irrational FDCs. 90 per cent of total retail sales are constituted of FDCs that are not mentioned in standard textbooks of medicines.[11]

In addition to incentivising the creation of irrational FDCs, price controls in India have discouraged manufacturers from producing certain products, causing shortages. A 2004 article in the British Medical Journal reported that, "drugs have become unavailable... and a black market - as well as spurious and counterfeit drugs - flourished." (Kumar, 2004.)

Patents

Some have claimed that patent protection in LDCs is a direct driver of counterfeit medicines. Such an argument is based on the premise that patents artificially drive up prices, thereby providing a significant opportunity for counterfeiters who only need to make a marginal profit over their production costs.

While theoretically plausible, this hypothesis has major flaws. First, as Amir Attaran has shown, more than 98 per cent of the WHO's Essential Medicines List is not patented in any poor country. Moreover, rights-holders rarely challenge patent infringements that take place in the poorest countries, particularly ARVs (Attaran, 2004). Second, most drugs sold in poor countries are off patent – and this pattern is reflected in the sales of counterfeits, suggesting that the price differential required to incentivize the production and distribution of fakes is small and that therefore the additional margin on patented medicines is not a relevant consideration in most cases.

What is being done?

This section discusses some of the main actions that are being taken by both governments and the private sector to address the problem of fake medicines.

In recent years, national governments and intergovernmental organisations have begun to develop policies to tackle the problem of fake medicines. While some of these measures may help, most are simply reactive and do not address the root causes described above.

One approach has been to increase spending on detection and seizure of counterfeit medicines. For example, between 2001 and 2006, authorities in Nigeria destroyed over $100 million worth of seized counterfeit medicines (Bate, 2008). Although each seizure has the positive effect of stopping counterfeit drugs reaching victims, its impact on the long-term problem is less clear. In spite of the series of high profile seizures by Nigerian National Agency for Food and Drug Administration and Control (NAFDAC), the vast trade in counterfeits appears to remain, with new cases constantly being discovered. As of December 2008 NAFDAC had seized and destroyed around N25 billion worth of counterfeit drugs and had 60 cases against accused perpetrators pending in courts.[12]

Similarly, NAFDAC regularly raids and sometimes closes down the large street markets where medicines are sold. Again, this does not address the root causes of the trade in counterfeit medicines. As long as consumers/patients lack reliable means of ensuring that the medicines they are buying are real, the incentive to sell counterfeits will remain – and vendors will find ways to sell them, circumventing measures through bribery or other criminal behaviour. Furthermore, closing down these markets affects the other non-drug related trading activities taking place, which are extremely important to local economies. Heavy-handed interventions between trading citizens is not a sustainable method of tackling counterfeiting.

Certain governments have suggested heftier criminal punishments for people involved in the trade in counterfeit medicines. In June 2008, laws against counterfeit drug trading were tightened in Peru, for example, with the introduction of a maximum sentence of ten years imprisonment for anyone found guilty of selling, storing, packaging or producing counterfeit medicines (Khond, 2008).

At the extreme end of this scale, India and China have introduced the death penalty for certain offences involving counterfeit drugs, though so far only China has actually invoked the penalty. In September 2008 the former head of the State Food and Drug Administration (SFDA) was executed after being convicted of accepting bribes to approve untested medicines.

While these measures suggest that powerful signals are being sent to those who produce and peddle counterfeit medicines, their actual effect may be counterproductive. Stronger criminal penalties will likely drive activities further into the hands of organised criminal cells. They will also likely result in further corruption, as the criminal cells seek to infiltrate lawenforcement agencies. Moreover, the introduction of mandatory Draconian punishments often has the effect of discouraging judges and juries from finding defendants guilty, because of the very serious consequence of making an incorrect decision, so may actually reduce the number of successful prosecutions.[13]

New regulators

In addition to imposing more Draconian penalties on those involved in the sale of counterfeit medicines, the governments of some countries have announced that they plan to create more expansive regulatory bodies. For instance, the Indian government announced in January 2008 the creation of a federal drug regulator.

The intention of such regulators is to overcome the problems created by weak – and often corrupt – regulators in certain states. However, as with the heftier penalties, the impact is not unambiguously positive.

First, extra layers of regulation create opportunities for bribery and corruption, especially in countries where the rule of law is weak. For example, in 2000 then-President of Nigeria Olusegun Obasanjo sacked the entire management of the National Agency for Food and Drug Administration and Control (NAFDAC), which had been established only seven years previously, due to evidence of corrupt practice. Likewise, in Italy in 2008 several senior officials from the country's drug regulatory agency were arrested in a 'cash-for-licenses' scandal.

Of course, the fact that these instances of corruption have come to light and their perpetrators dealt with is a positive sign, suggesting that perhaps in future corruption will be less of a problem.

However, to the extent that control of corruption rests on political intervention, there is a danger that as power changes hands, such controls will not be applied so rigorously. Worse, the ability to remove corrupt officials may itself be applied in a corrupt manner, furthering the interests of those in power and their supporters, which might include manufacturers of fake medicines, rendering the legislation counterproductive.

A further problem with drug regulators is that they (inevitably) delay access to new drugs. In the US, regulatory approval for new medicines typically takes between 12 and 24 months. In South Africa, new drugs that have already been passed by regulators in the US or EU face delays of up to two years at the hands of the Medicines Control Agency. This creates yet more gaps in supply to be exploited by counterfeiters.

Identity preservation technologies

The manufacturers and distributors of high quality branded medicines have strong incentives to act against counterfeit and substandard medicine because such fakes remove legitimate business and harm the reputations of their brands. Unsurprisingly therefore, both pharmaceutical companies and retailers are taking steps to address the problem.

Early attempts by the private sector to prevent counterfeiting focused on the use of trademarked branding, combined with idiosyncratic pill shapes and colours. Later on, tamper-evident packaging systems were introduced. Gradually, more sophisticated measures were taken, including the use of holographic images on packaging. However, even these have now been copied by counterfeiters, so more drastic measures are necessary. Current efforts focus on mass serialisation systems, using technologies based on barcodes, RFID tag systems or simple scratch panels. It is believed that such systems are sufficiently complex to render any attempts at counterfeiting extremely uneconomical.

End-to-end technologies

Mobile phones are now so sufficiently widespread in LDCs that access can be considered near-universal. This has enabled the development of a range of technologies that enable purchasers of medicines to check the authenticity of their packs using text message (SMS) services. The systems rely on a unique identifying code in the form of a simple series of numbers, which is printed on the pack and then concealed. When the packet is bought, the purchaser scratches off the concealing panel to reveal the code and then sends the code by SMS to a central registry, which contains a copy of each code made for that medicine. If the code is unique, then the purchaser will shortly receive an SMS response informing them that the medicine is real. If the code is not in the system or is not unique, then they will be told that the medicine is likely to be a counterfeit. Such SMS systems have been developed in Ghana, India and the USA, and are currently being offered across Africa and Asia.

Supplier to pharmacy technologies

The SMS systems described above seek to ensure that the identity of a product is preserved from the time it leaves the manufacturer to the time it is purchased by the end 'consumer' (which in most cases will be the patient, but might be a relative or friend). Other services have been developed which focus on other points in the supply chain - in particular retail pharmacies.

Like the end-to-end SMS system, most use codes to identify packages of medicines. The specific coding systems vary, however, with some using a number (as with the SMS system), some use a bar code (which is scanned and sent to a central registry for evaluation), while some use radio-frequency identification (RFID).

Scientists are developing methods of labelling and serialising products that are increasingly difficult for counterfeiters to circumvent. One further example of this is DNA coding, in which synthetically produced strands of DNA are fitted into a label and a checking device. This can be used to check that products are genuine all through the supply chain, as can RFID. The latter has the advantage of being able to check devices quickly as they pass and is the same technology as used, for example, with travel cards on some public transport systems. It is, however, expensive when compared to barcodes and scratch panels, and there are concerns that the heating effect of RFID can affect covalent bonds in protein and biologic products. The FDA in America has therefore advised against using RFID tags on biologics and protein drugs.

State-supported serialization

Most of the technologies described above have emerged through private organisations simply responding to the problem of counterfeit medicines - without prompting or intervention from government. Yet their success is now resulting in calls for governments to require specific technologies. For instance, the state of California has already passed legislation to mandate use of a comprehensive 'track and trace' system. Such measures, again, may be well-meaning, but can in fact cause more harm than good.

Mandatory requirements can place excessive costs on small businesses, acting as a barrier to entry and protecting larger companies from competition. For example, small pharmacies in California could face costs of between $84,000 and $110,000 to implement the first year of the 'track and trace' system. Meanwhile the EU's latest proposals admits "pharmacies are going to bear costs of approximately Euro 7157 million", with up to 711 billion of costs falling on manufacturers and importers of medicinal products. [14]

Furthermore, by laying down specific technological requirements, such regulations will entrench those technologies that happen to be favoured by officials at a particular time. This will crowd out the spontaneous development of alternative, innovative technologies, undermining competition and stifling further innovation. To the extent that these technologies are themselves susceptible to fraud and counterfeiting (e.g. through hacking of the computer systems utilised to convey information), such mandates could ultimately be counterproductive. If end-to-end technologies are successful, there is no need for governments to attempt to track the entire supply chain.

Conclusion

The fight against fake medicines has the advantage that many criminals involved are unlikely to have a particular commitment to this activity. At present it is simply an easy and convenient way to make money. By addressing the root causes that enable such profitable opportunities, their incentives can be diminished, thereby reclaiming the market for high quality medicines.

This chapter suggests that the supply of fake drugs could be considerably reduced by:

1. Strengthening local institutions, in particular the rule of law;
2. Governments intervening less in the pharmaceutical market;
3. Better use of technologies for identity preservation.

The most fundamental cause of the spread of fake drugs in less developed countries has been the inability of manufacturers to protect the identity of their products. This is largely down to a lack of functioning rule of law, which makes it very difficult for manufacturers to protect their trademarks and brands - thereby handing a free rein to counterfeiters. In this context, the stiffer criminal penalties called for by the WHO and other bodies may actually entrench the corrupt symbiotic relationship between counterfeiters, lawmakers and officials.

Many existing licensing systems for pharmaceuticals in LDCs serve practically no purpose other than to restrict the sale of legitimate products manufactured by foreign companies. As such, they offer a boon to suppliers of fakes. However, we are cautious about the introduction of stronger and more rigorous regulations, since these are likely to add significantly to the cost and time it takes to bring new medicines to market, thereby providing further gaps in the market for fakers to exploit. And if such regulations are applied in an arbitrary and corrupt manner, they may end up being counterproductive; undermining rather than improving confidence in the pharmaceutical supply chain.

Although highly desirable from the perspective of wider economic development, bolstering the rule of law in LDCs is a long-term and uncertain process. We must therefore consider the most effective steps that can be taken in the short-term. Happily, those in the best position to secure the integrity of branded pharmaceuticals (both patented and generic), namely the manufacturers, are already taking steps in this direction. The private sector should take advantage of its innovative capacity to experiment with different technological solutions to brand infringement. It is well-placed to lead this process, as it has unparalleled access to the entire pharmaceutical supply chain, as well as the clear financial incentive to protect its revenue.

Governments also have a role to play beyond improving the rule of law. Many government interventions in the pharmaceutical market have restricted supplies of quality medicines, driving up prices and simply leading to gaps in the market. These have then been exploited by purveyors of fake medicines. Governments could substantially reduce these problems by removing impediments to the supply of quality medicines, such as taxes, tariffs, price controls and arbitrary regulations.

Notes

1. President, International Policy Network, United Kingdom.
2. Independent researcher.
3. Executive Director, Emerging Markets Health Network.
4. Available at www.psi-inc.org, PSI's annual Situation Report.
5. European Commission Taxation and Custom Union (TAXUD) statistics, 2005.
6. "Fake drug industry operates openly", LiveMint, 13th May 2007 http://www.livemint.com/2007/04/30000718/Fake-drug-industryoperates-op.html [Accessed 6th April 2009]
7. The WHO estimates that 200,000 - 300,000 people die each year in China due to fake medicines, while the European Commission's 2006 report estimated that 20% of fake drug imports come from China (European Commission Taxation and Customs Union, "Summary of Community Customs Activities on Counterfeit and Piracy").
8. Available at http://www.blogher.com/chinese-parents-filing-lawsuits-over-milk-contaminated-deaths.
9. Confederation of Indian Industry booklet, *Technology Solutions; A Primer for Combating Counterfeiting and Piracy* (December 2008)
10. Available at http://www.livemint.com/2007/08/19235926/Combination-drugs-set-to-lose.html, "The Menace of Combo Drugs." India: Deccan Herald. <Available online at www.deccanherald.com/Content/Apr32008/editpage2008040260701.asp; "40 fixed-dose-combination drugs may be off chemists' shelves." India: Business Line. <Available online at http://www.thehindubusinessline.com/2007/09/04/ stories/2007090451011100.htm>
11. Available at http://www.karmayog.org/redirect/strred. asp?docId=15364, http://www.essentialdrugs.org/ edrug/archive/200804/msg00004. php.
12. "NAFDAC destroys N24.25b counterfeit drugs in seven years", http://www.ngrguardiannews.com/ business/article02/indexn2_html?pdate=241208&ptitle =NAFDAC%20 destroys%20N24.25b%20counterfeit%20drugs%20 in%20seven%20years
13. There is evidence of this in other contexts. For example, juries acquitting defendants in cases for which the mandatory sentence was death. See e.g. Foley (2003) at p. 99.

14 Available at http://eur-lex.europa.eu/LexUriServ LexUriServ. do?uri= COM:2008:0668:FIN:EN:HTML,

Bibliography

Alter Hall, K., Newton, P. N., Green, M. D., De Veij, M., Vandenabeele, P., Pizzanelli, D., Mayxay, M., Dondorp, A., Fernandez, F. M. (2006), "Characterization of Counterfeit Artesunate Antimalarial tablets from SE Asia", *American Journal of Tropical Medicine and Hygiene*, 75(5): 804-811.

Amin, A, Snow, R, Kolwaro, G. (2005), "The quality of sulphadoxinepyrimethane and amodaquine products in the Kenyan retail sector", *Journal of Clinical Pharmacological Therapy*, 30: 559-565.

Bate, Roger (2008), "Making a Killing", Washington, DC: The American Enterprise Institute Press.

Bate, R., Coticelli, P., Tren, R., Attaran, A. (2008), "Antimalarial Drug Quality in the Most Severely Malarious Parts of Africa - A Six Country Study", PLoS One (Public Library of Science), available at http://www.plosone.org/article/ info:doi%2F10.1371% 2Fjournal.pone.0002132>

Bate, R., Tren, R., Mooney, L., Boateng, K. (2006), "Tariffs, Corruption and Other Impediments to Medicinal Access in Developing Countries: Field Evidence", Washington, DC: American Enterprise Institute, Working Paper 130.

Bate, Roger, Richard Tren, Jasson Urbach (2005), "Still Taxed to Death: An Analysis of Taxes and Tariffs on Medicines, Vaccines and Medical Devices", Washington, DC: American Enterprise Institute - Brookings Joint Centre for Regulatory Studies.

Bogdanich, W., Hooker, J. (2007), "From China to Panama, a Trail of Poisoned Medicine", New York: New York Times, available at http://www.nytimes. com/2007/05/06/world/06poison.html?_ r=2&hp&ore f=slogin&oref=slogin>

Choudhury, M (2004), "Quality assessment of some paedriatric cotrimoxazole suspensions marketed in Bangladesh", *Hamdard Medicus*I (2):58–62.

Clark, Eric (2008), "The pills that kill", London: Daily Telegraph.

Confederation of Indian Industry (2008), "Technology Solutions: a primer for combating counterfeiting and piracy", New Delhi.

EFPIA (undated), "Pharma industry leaders call for strong EU measures to combat counterfeit medicines, including a ban on medicine repackaging", EurActive. available at http://pr.euractiv.com/?q=node/3811.

Foley, M.A. (2003), *Arbitrary and capricious: the supreme court, the constitution, and the death penalty.* Westport, CT: Praeger

Gaudiano, M. C., Di Maggio, A., Cocchieri, E., Antoniella, E., Bertocchi, P., Alimonti, S., Valvo, L. (2007), "Medicines Informal Market in Congo, Burundi and Angola: Counterfeit and Sub-Standard Antimalarials" *Malaria Journal*, 6(22).

Gibb, G. (2008), "Deaths Linked to Contaminated Heparin Soar to 62", Washington, DC: available at http://www.lawyersandsettlements.com/articles/10401/heparin-deaths-soar.html

Hogerzeil, H., V., Battersby, A., Srdanovic, V., Stjernstrom, N., E. (1992), "Stability of essential drugs during shipment to the tropics", *British Medical Journal*, 304(6821): 210–212.

Hogerzeil, H., V., De Goeje, M., J., Abu Reid, I., O. (1991), "Stability of essential drugs in Sudan", *The Lancet*, 338:754–755.

Juan, Shan (2008), "Irregularities found in samples of lethal drugs", *China Daily*, available at http:// www.chinadaily.com.cn/china/2008-06/03/ content_6729905.htm

Kelesidis, T., Kelesidis, I., Rafailidis, P., I., Falagas, M., E. (2007), "Counterfeit or substandard antimicrobial drugs: a review of the scientific evidence", *Journal of Antimicrobial Chemotherapy*, 60(2):214-36.

Khond, Pragati (2008), "Up To 10 Year Imprisonment For Drug Counterfeiters In Peru", India: The Med Guru, available at http://www.themedguru.com/ articles/up_to_10_year_ imprisonment_for_drug_ counterfeiters_in_peru-7324138.html

Kumar, S. (2004), "India to extend price controls on drugs", *British Medical Journal*, 14; 329(7462): 368.

Kotwani, A., Levison, L. (2007), "Price components and access to medicines in Delhi, India".

Laing, Richard and Muge Olcay (2005), "Pharmaceutical Tariffs: What is their effect on prices, protection of local industry and revenue generation?" The Commission on Intellectual Property Rights, Innovation and Public Health, World Health Organization.

Lal, Neeta (2008), "Fake Drugs a Bitter Pill for India", available at http://www.atimes.com/atimes/ South_Asia/JF07Df01.html

Levison, L. & Laing, R. (2003), "The hidden costs of essential medicines," *WHO essential drugs monitor*, 33.

Macaleer, Andy (2008), "The State of the Pharmaceutical Supply Chain Safety and Security", New Jersey: Advantage Business Media, available at http://www.pharmpro.com/ShowPR.aspx?PUB CODE=021& ACCT=0000100&ISSUE=0806&RELTYPE= ATO& PRODCODE=0000& PRODLETT=AC&CommonCount=0>

Maureen Lewis (2006), "Governance and Corruption in Public Health Care Systems", Center for Global Development, Working Paper Number 78, January.

Maya, C. (2007), "Central directive to ban sale of 1,105 brands of drugs" India: The Hindu, available at http://www.hindu.com/2007/07/02/ stories/2007070254160400.htm

McGivering, Jill (2007), "Tracking the fake malaria drug threat", BBC News, available at http://news.bbc. co.uk/1/hi/world/asia-pacific/ 6692431.stm

Megget, Katrna (2008), "Sweden launches a TV campaign to warn about fake drugs", Pharma Times, available at http://www.ifpma.org/ PressReviewEmail/ PressReviewDetail. aspx?nID=10771&SD= wULU5Fc5Xh 1xC0zG19IDbA%3d%3d>

Miller, Henry (2008), "Poison Pills", London: The Guardian, available at http://commentisfree. guardian.co.uk/henry_miller/2008/04/ poison_pills.html

Nazerali, H., Muchemwa, T., Hogerzeil, H., V. (1996), "Stability of Essential Drugs in Tropical Climates: Zimbabwe", EDM Research Series Number 13, World Health Organization.

Newton, Paul et al. (2008), "A Collaborative Epidemiological Investigation Into the Criminal Fake Artesunate Trade in South East Asia", *PLoS Med.*, 5(2): 52.

Newton, Paul (2007), "Counterfeit Artemisinin Derivatives and Africa", PLoS Med 4(3): 139.

Okeke, I., N., Lamikanra, A., Edelman, R. (1999), "Socioeconomic and Behavioral Factors Leading to Acquired Bacterial Resistance to Antibiotics in Developing Countries", *Emerging Infectious Diseases*, 5 (1): 18–27.

Pescov, Alexei (2008), "Counterfeit Drugs: A Threat to Russia's Security", Moscow News, available at http://www.mnweekly.ru/national/ 20080610/55332994. html

Pitts, Peter (2006), "Counterfeit Drugs and China", Center for Medicines in the Public Interest, available at http://www.cmpi.org/testimony/[fake/counterfeit]- drugs-and-china

Shleifer, A., and Vishny R. (1993), "Corruption." *Quarterly Journal of Economics* 108(3): 599–617.

Sow, P. S., Gueye, T. S. N., Sy, E., Toure, L., Ba, C., Badiane, M. (2002), "Drugs in the Parallel Market for the Treatment of Urethral Discharge in Dakar: Epidemiological Investigation Physiochemical Tests," *International Journal of Infectious Diseases,* 6 (2): 108–12.

Stevens, Philip (2003), "Fighting the Diseases of Poverty", New Jersey: Transaction Publishers.

Taylor, L. (2008), "UK launches new drug access alliance for Third World", London: Pharma Times.

Tipke, M., Diallo, S., Coulibaly, B., Störzinger, D., Hoppe- Tichy, T., Sie, A., Müller Tipke, O. (2008), "Substandard antimalarial drugs in Burkina Faso", *Malaria Journal* (May).

Tren, R, (2005), "Price controls reduce the availability of medicines", South Africa, the Free Market Foundation.

Underwood, Mitya (2008), "Jail threat for fake medicine", United Arab Eremites: The National, available at http://www.thenational.ae/article/20080529/NATIONA L/573216782/1001&profile=1001.

WHO (2007), "Press Release", Oct 17th, Geneva: World Health Organization.

World Health Organization (2006), "Factsheet 2006", available at http://www.who.int/mediacentre/factsheets/ fs275/en

WHO Review (2005), "Review of Malaria Drug Efficacy Situation in 10 Countries", available at http:// www.wpro.who.int/NR/rdonlyres/EB88557E-C21F- 41E0-9DD9-801C00968794/0/ Reviewofthe MalariaDrugEfficacy.pdf

Who Report (2008), "Global Malaria Control and Elimination", available at http://www.who.int/ malaria/docs/drugresistance/Malaria_Artemisinin. pdf

World Health Organization (2008), "Anti-Tuberculosis drug resistance in the world; fourth global report", available at http:// www.who.int/tb/publications/2008/drs_report4_26feb08.pdf (accessed March 2009).

Wongsrichanalai, Meshnick (2008), "Declining Artesunate-Mefloquine Efficacy against Falciparum Malaria on the Cambodia-Thailand Border", available at http://www.cdc.gov/EID/content/14/5/716.htm.

5

Who Benefits from India's Attempts to Control Drug Prices through Compulsion?

Amir Ullah Khan[1]

The healthcare system

India's failing public health system was in the spotlight again when UNICEF's 'Child Mortality Estimates Report 2012' recorded that in 2011, 50 per cent of global under-five deaths occurred in just five countries: India, Nigeria, the Democratic Republic of the Congo, Pakistan and China. India's toll is higher than the deaths in Nigeria, Democratic Republic of Congo and Pakistan put together.

In the South Asian region, life expectancy at birth of 64 years in India is only higher than 63 in Nepal. The gap between India and Sri Lanka keeps growing as life expectancy in the island country is now 75. The infant mortality rate in India at 56 per 1,000 live births (111 in Madhya Pradesh and 17 in Kerala) is better than that of only Pakistan. In Sri Lanka, meanwhile only 12 children in every 1000 live births die in infancy. The question that is therefore being asked in India in many circles is whether the government should be responsible for extending complete health coverage to its citizens.

It is also true that nearly two thirds of India's population lacks access to clean drinking water and sanitation. As a result, the country has a high burden of communicable diseases like diarrhea, hepatitis, cholera and typhoid. In another widely publicized report released by the Indian Prime Minister, the Naandi foundation has estimated that 59 per cent of our children are stunted, which means they have been suffering from malnutrition for a long period of time resulting in low height for the child's age, while 42 per cent are underweight. Once again the ratio of such children is higher among Scheduled Tribes, Scheduled castes and Muslims than among the general population.

There is a direct correlation between child malnutrition and the economic and social status, educational level of mothers, awareness of the advantages of hand washing and sanitary hygiene. The Prime Minister declared that it was unacceptable that such acute and miserable conditions exist despite sustained economic growth over several decades. What is alarming is that the numbers of children suffering from stunting, wasting and general malnutrition in India is more than double the proportion in the poorest parts of sub Saharan Africa.

The issue is whether it is enough to provide a reasonable amount of heath care service to a certain proportion of the population? In other words, should the government be responsible for Universal Health coverage[2]? The debate has also been on strategies of developing the health system and achieving universal coverage. This is revolves around two streams of thought - on the supply side, a strengthening of the public healthcare system so that low-cost healthcare is made available, and on the demand-side focusing on financing by promoting universal health insurance programmes, where government funds the premium for the poor. Are the two strategies mutually exclusive for a vast and diverse country like India? Having experimented with various options, the Planning Commission seems to have come around again to the view that it is the state that must guarantee access to health care to all. The enormous expense of such an undertaking is placing massive pressure on reducing drug prices. By any means possible! Patented medicines made by foreign companies are a politically attractive place to start- even though they make up less than 10% of the overall pharmaceutical market in India. Hence the recent compulsory licenses issued against the products of foreign manufacturers.

The Intellectual Property Rights institution

The most popular form of intellectual property is the copyright where the producer of artistic and literary works gets the sole right to publish and sell her work. The other major form of intellectual property is the patent[3]. Drug companies own patents over the medicine they have invented and this prevents others from manufacturing the same drug, unless the patent has expired. Patent law says that owners have a monopoly over the invention for 20 years, after which the formula, the flowchart and the recipe becomes public knowledge and anyone can manufacture the item.

Therefore those who spend millions of dollars on their research and development must earn back their investment within the 20 year period that the patent law allows them. The big drug firms argue that they are able to invent new drugs because they spend millions and sometimes billions in developing new drugs. It takes around eight years to go through the various phases of drug research, including genetic analysis, animal testing, and clinical trials on human patients. All this requires large investments, and the time taken to go through these research and approval stages eats into the twenty year monopoly period granted by the original patent. On average, a patented drug has only twelve to thirteen years exclusivity on the market before it is exposed to generic competition (Adams & Brantner, 2003; Dranove and Meltzer, 1994).

Table 1: Duration and success rate for new chemical drugs

	Pre-clinical	*Phase 1*	*Phase 2*	*Phase 3 and regulatory approval*	*Total*
Probability of success (%)	0.1	80.7	57.7	56.7	0.03
Successful duration (in months)	42	19.7	29.9	47	96.6

Source: Abrantes-Metz et al (2004)

The business of drug research is also very high risk, with less than one in a thousand initial researching a new drugs making it past the first stage of pre-clinical trials. The costs of these many thousands of failed investigations and trials must be factored into the price of those few drugs that do eventually make it to the market (Table 1). Those few drugs that gain marketing approval from the regulator are therefore usually sold for high prices, to recover sunk costs and to then create a corpus for the next drug that must be invented.

The high costs of drug development are at the root of current controversies around drug pricing in India. Many argue that if drugs are very expensive, then the poor would never be able to afford them and they will die. Therefore they urge their governments to ensure that patented drugs are sold at an affordable price. Drug firms, meanwhile, argue that unless they are free to price their drugs as they see fit, they will not be able to generate sufficient returns to reinvest in R&D, and future innovation will cease. The Indian government has firmly come down against the argument of foreign drug companies, and on the side of its domestic generic drug industry, which stands to benefit from these licenses.

Flexibility through Compulsory licenses[4]

This debate has also been playing out for many years at the international level. The TRIPS (Trade Related Intellectual Property Rights) agreement under the World Trade Organization, ensures that each member country must respect the patent rights of all citizens of all member countries. However TRIPS maintains that while intellectual property protection is important for the development of new medicines, there are genuine concerns about its effects on prices. There is also a consensus the TRIPS Agreement does not and should not prevent Members from taking measures to protect public health. Each Member has the right to grant compulsory licenses and the freedom to determine the grounds upon which such licenses are granted.

Flexibilities such as "parallel importation"[5] and "compulsory licensing" are written into the TRIPS Agreement – governments can issue compulsory licenses to allow other companies to make a patented product or use a patented process under license without the consent of the patent owner, but only under certain conditions aimed at safeguarding the legitimate interests of the patent holder. Article 31(f) of the Trade-Related Aspects of Intellectual Property Rights (TRIPS) Agreement says that production under compulsory licensing must be predominantly for the domestic market.

The Indian law on Patents allows compulsory licensing when "the patented invention is not available to the public at an affordable and reasonable price". However Indian pharmaceutical companies do not spend much on R&D, so their costs are very low. The actual figure is 1-2% of drug sales, as compared to figures of 15% in Europe and North America and 10% in Japan. Thus, stronger patent protection tends to encourage R&D, apart from stimulating foreign direct investments into the sector, which also stimulates R&D efforts. The cost of developing a new drug is estimated to be at least 125 million US dollars, with some estimates going up to 1 billion US dollars. Given this kind of figure and given the low level of R&D expenditure by most Indian pharmaceutical companies, they will always argue for copying inventions from the West and then try to get compulsory licenses from the government.

Natco Pharmaceuticals in Hyderabad got a big gift from the Indian patent Office in early 2012 when it was granted a compulsory license to manufacture and sell a patented cancer drug Nexavar that belongs to Bayer. Bayer sells this drug that fights kidney and liver cancer for 5698 US dollars or Rs 284,428 rupees for a month's dosage. Natco Pharma Ltd. has promised to supply the same drug for a month for 178 US dollars or Rs 8,800 rupees if allowed to. The ruling of the Indian patent office now compulsorily takes away the monopoly right that Bayer, the inventor of Nexavar has, and gives it to Natco to make the drug accessible to more people.

The ruling therefore raises a serious issue. Does the government have the right to take away the ownership of any intellectual property and give it to someone who is not the inventor to manufacture? Any new manufacturer who has not spent money and effort in inventing a new drug will of course be able to supply it for a far lesser cost. The government has taken the stance that if firms that take patents on drugs and do not then bring them to India within three years, they must allow local industry to manufacture the drug and pay the owner some royalty. In this case, Natco will pay Bayer 6% royalty.

This is a serious issue that needs to be first understood and then debated widely. The foundation for this debate is the broader concept of intellectual property and the specific issue of patent rights. Intellectual property rights are ownership rights given to those who produce intangible goods that emerge from the mind and acquire some commercial value. In the Indian context, there is enough evidence to show that free access to foreign technology has led to a general atmosphere of plagiarism and copying, which has undermined India's potential for driving economic growth through innovation.

The domestic pharmaceutical industry had free access to foreign technology in the period between 1970 and 2005 when the country did not recognize patent rights and therefore it was easier for the industry to either blatantly copy technology or alter it a bit and manufacture products developed abroad. Free access to foreign technology, in the face of poor IPR implementation, has enabled Indian industry to succumb to the temptation of using foreign technology, tinkering with it and adapting it with minor changes to suit the Indian market. Coupled with licensing and entry barriers, this policy has ensured that most of the manufacturing sector has remained backward, capital intensive and technologically archaic.[6]

While this case against Bayer will be argued for by various experts who will call this a victory for Indian patients, it must be borne in mind that these are unilateral decisions that do not respect property rights, and undermine the rule of law. In any case, Natco's proposed price of 8000 rupees a month, amounting to about 160 USD, is not affordable for the poor or indeed most of the middle-class.

In a country like India which already suffers from a poor reputation in protecting property rights of all owners of land and buildings, this example will only make the investor wary of coming here. These real costs must be weighed against the fact that such compulsory licenses will do little to help address the real causes of India's healthcare problems, which revolve around poor sanitation, malnutrition and weak healthcare infrastructure.

In conclusion

Current Indian legislation has several sections on compulsory licensing. For example, Compulsory licensing is possible after three years after the grant of the patent and it can only be used "..........when the reasonable requirements of the public with respect to the patented invention have not been satisfied" and "......the patented invention is not available to the public at a reasonable price". Compulsory licenses are to be granted only if efforts have been made to obtain authorization from the right holder on reasonable terms and conditions and such efforts have not been successful. The government has wide-ranging powers in granting compulsory licenses, which also do not provide the patent holder any hearing. There ought to be a judicial review of any decision to revoke or forfeit a patent. Since importation is regarded as equivalent to the working of a patent, the failure to import is the only legitimate condition for the issue of a compulsory license.

Compulsory licensing, permitted only for items of public non-commercial use and in national emergencies, should have only been resorted to on the merits of each case. In the normal course of the development of the law under IPRs, what actually should have happened is a depending of the difficulties in resorting to compulsory licensing. In issuing the compulsory license on Bayer's product, the Controller of Patents has taken none of these concerns into account, and is behaving in an arbitrary manner that is inconsistent with the rule of law. The discretionary powers appropriated by the Controller of Patents should have been rendered void long ago. And it is critical to remember that even after the license has been issued, the patent holder retains the right to be heard and there cannot be any discrimination between domestic producer and imported goods.

All intellectual property regimes must manage a fine balance between encouraging innovation and making those innovations affordable to as many as possible. Many foreign companies in a range of innovative sectors are looking to emerging markets like India to boost sales as their revenues decline in home markets. By this reckoning, the costs future innovation will be increasingly underwritten by emerging markets, as consumers and governments in the West retrench. The future of foreign investment in innovative R&D activities is therefore heavily dependent on the attitude of governments such as India's attitude to property rights. This case will also determine the future trajectory of the Indian industry, in particular whether it will continue with its current model of low value-added copying. This is why the Bayer/Natco case is of international significance.

Notes

1. Amir Ullah Khan is an economist working on trade policy issues.
2. A high level group expert group on Universal Health coverage for India submitted its report to the Planning Commission in November of 2011 to bring the discussion on healthcare firmly back on the table. The report puts a large amount of data out to establish the context in which this issue becomes alarming.
3. A patent is the right given to an inventor who produces something that is new and useful. The patent holder therefore is a monopoly who then makes money from selling the new invention or by licensing its manufacture to someone else. The most well-known inventor who

earned his livelihood from inventing and then patenting his inventions was Thomas Alva Edison and his most famous patent was on the light bulb.

4. Also referred to as Authorizations for Government Approved generic copies or the compelled relaxation of an intellectual property rights owners' right to exclude in exchange for a licensee's payments. Cahoy, *Confronting myths and Myopia on the road to Doha.*

5. Patenting gives to the patentee an exclusive right over the product. However, exhaustion of intellectual property rights implies that this exclusive right to import the protected product is exhausted, and ends, when the product is launched in the market. Any country that then applies this principle of exhaustion in terms of its intellectual property rights validates and approves parallel importation for everyone in the country.

6. S. Jacobson, "Government Policy and Performance of the Indian Engineering Industry", Research Policy, February 1991.

References

Abrantes-Metz, R., Adams, C. and Metz A. (2004), "Pharmaceutical Development Phases: A Duration Analysis", Federal Trade Commission, Working Paper #274.

Adams, C. and Brantner, V. (2003) "New Drug Development: Estimating Entry form Human Clinical Trials", Federal Trade Commission, Working Paper #262.

Bird, Robert, and Daniel R. Cahoy. (2008), "The Impact of Compulsory Licensing on Foreign Direct Investment: A Collective Bargaining Approach", *American Business Law Journal*, 45(2): 283-330.

Danzon, Patricia M., and Li-Wei Chao (2000), "Does Regulation Drive Out Competition in Pharmaceutical Markets?", *The Journal of Law and Economics*, 43(2): 311-358.

Drahos, Peter. (2004), "Intellectual property and pharmaceutical markets: a nodal governance approach." *Temp. L. Rev.* 77: 401.

Dranover, D. & Meltzer, D. (1994), "Do Important Drugs Reach the Market Sooner?", *The RAND Journal of Economics*, 25(3):402–423

Frank, Richard G. (2003), "New estimates of drug development costs." *Journal of Health Economics*, 22(2): 325-330.

Keayla, B.K. (1994), "Patent Protection and the Pharmaceutical Industry", in K.R.G. Nair and Ashok Kumar edited, *Intellectual Property Rights*, Allied Publishers, Delhi.

Love, James, and Tim Hubbard (2004), "Make drugs affordable: replace TRIPs-plus by R&D-plus", *Bridges*, 8: 1-4.

Maria Burke (1996), "Getting into bed with Biotech", *Chemistry and Industry*, March.

N Lalitha (2002), "Indian Pharmaceutical Industry in WTO Regime-A SWOT Analysis", *Economic and Political Weekly*, 37(34): 3542-3555.

Naandi Foundation (2011), "Hungama Survey report", available at http://www.naandi.org/1008569_Hungama_Bk.pdf

Rozek, Richard P. (2000), "The effects of compulsory licensing on innovation and access to health care", *The Journal of World Intellectual Property*, 3(6): 889-917.

Tandon, Pankaj (1982), "Optimal patents with compulsory licensing", *The Journal of Political Economy*, 90(3): 470-486.

Velasquez, German, Piya Hanvoravongchai, and Pascale Boulet (2001), "Globalization, patents and drugs: an annotated bibliography".

6

The Role of the Private Sector in Achieving Universal Health Coverage in Asia and Beyond

Philip Stevens

As populations in middle and low-income countries become wealthier as a result of globalisation and economic liberalisation, many governments are now placing an increased focus on improving the provision of social welfare services such as health and education. Countries such as China and India have for many years struggled to provide health services that are affordable, high quality and available, particularly for those on low-income or in rural areas. As a result, there is a new focus on the provision of 'Universal Health Care', with many countries enacting new legislation to guarantee a 'right' to healthcare for citizens, and reforming structures to bolster public sector provision of care.

China announced an overhaul of its health system in 2009 to bring safe, affordable basic health services to all residents, committing about $126 billion to reform the quality and efficiency of its health care. Achieving Universal Healthcare is a widely-shared political aim in India, and in 2012 the Planning

Commission's High Level Expert Group stated this could only be achieved by far greater public spending, a centralisation of services and strengthening of public-sector health institutions.[1]

This state-centric approach does not inspire optimism, given its well-documented failures in many other sectors including agriculture, retail, manufacturing, and natural resource-extraction. Although the United States is currently in the process of increasing the role of government in healthcare provision, other countries (including the United Kingdom) are retreating from centrally-directed government healthcare monopolies, and exploring new approaches that embrace competition, choice and other mechanisms of accountability for providers.

Such state-centric approaches are especially ill-suited to emerging economies. Most ministries of health in low and middle-income countries do not have the capacity, expertise, logistical skills, or incentives to deliver a complex service like healthcare to every citizen. Although advances in resource tracking within the health systems of developing countries have been made recently, many health systems lack sufficient auditing procedures and public expenditure management systems (Powell-Jackson & Mills, 2007), making it difficult for government administrators to do their jobs effectively.

This lack of financial accountability creates an environment in which corruption can thrive, particularly in countries that suffer from a weak rule of law. Corruption occurs at many levels, including direct embezzlement at the ministerial level; fraud in billing; local medical staff selling "free" drugs on the grey market, institutionalised absenteeism, and illegal payments to health care personnel that allow patients to jump queues or obtain treatment (Lewis, 2006; Transparency International, 2006).

Alternative strategies – making greater use of the private sector

The failures of the current approach are not attributable to weaknesses within the public sector *per se*. Rather, it is largely attributable to the misalignment of incentives faced by public health bureaucracies. In general, public sector healthcare in lower-income countries is heavily centralised, with ministers and officials in the centre planning the location of services, and decreeing by diktat the activities of medical personnel. As a result, public health services tend to be unresponsive to local demand, with practitioners answerable to their bureaucratic masters rather than the people they are supposed to be serving. This lack of direct accountability leaves enormous scope for corruption. The situation is compounded by the fact that most health ministries tend to favour input-based payment to local providers, taking the form of lump-sum grants, or payment depending on numbers of staff or size of facilities. Western donors have compounded this structural problem by promulgating 'no strings' direct transfers to governments, rather than working to promote more decentralised forms of health provision. These factors create an environment in which those involved in the delivery of healthcare have little incentive beyond altruism to provide high quality care to patients.

While the strengthening of state-centric approaches is much in vogue amongst international agencies such as WHO, and major governments such as India and China, there is a strong case for examining other, more decentralised forms of health support that offer the potential to both reduce costs and improve patient care. Fortunately, an alternative to the current system already exists in the form of an enormous and diverse private health sector within lower and middle-income countries, which already provides the majority of treatment for the poor. According to International Finance Corporation and World Bank figures, between one-third and one-half of the US$16.7 billion spent on health care in sub-Saharan Africa in 2005 was spent in the private sector, often by the poorest people who cannot get government services (International Finance Corporation, 2007). In Asia the private sector provides 26 per cent of all hospital beds, with this figure rising to 33 per cent in Africa (Hanson & Berman, 1998). In India, about 80% of care is provided by the private sector (Rockefeller Foundation, 2008). Governments frequently do nothing to harness this massive capacity, leaving the poor to pay for private health care out of their own pockets, with obvious and well-documented ramifications for equity and affordability.

There has already been some experimentation with the use of the private sector in many countries, which may provide some pointers about how to scale up treatment and prevention for chronic disease. This chapter examines models of private sector experimentation for healthcare provision. It firstly focuses on supply-side models, which involve the private sector delivering health services to patients, and then turns to demand-side interventions, which increase the ability of patients to access those services. These latter mechanisms include methods of funding access to health services on behalf of patients, particularly the poorest.

Table 1: Models involving the Private Sector

Supply-side	*Demand-side*
Social franchising	Health Equity funds
Contracting	Microfinance / community health insurance
Public private partnerships	Private health insurance
Pure private provision	

Private sector health delivery - supply side approaches

Franchising

Opponents of the use of the private sector for delivering healthcare in low and middle-income countries often argue that its quality is too variable to be reliable. While many private sector organisations maintain the highest standards (for example, Indian private hospitals), other private sector participants are simply "one man bands" that operate outside the purview of regulators.

One way of improving quality and lowering costs is through the use of social franchising, in which different independent health providers are commissioned to provide services under an established, unifying brand at specified prices and standards. This harmonises things such as training and procurement and thereby achieves savings from economies of scale. For franchisees, it opens up new revenue streams and access to drugs, training and laboratories. It also places considerable pressure on them to adhere to the quality standards stipulated by the franchisor: if those standards are not met, the franchise will not be renewed. Franchises can be either commercial or social in their motivation, and by harnessing the capacity of the private sector, they offer the potential for governments to increase considerably the quality and quantity of health provision.

Franchises for health services have been used successfully in a wide variety of geographical and social contexts, ranging from providing sexual health services to truck drivers in India, to training midwives in the Philippines (Prata et al, 2005).

There are a number of criteria that must be met for them to be successful: there must be spare capacity in the medical sector; franchise networks must be large enough to benefit from economies of scale in advertising and monitoring; the services being offered must be sufficiently definable so they can be offered at a standardised and auditable quality; and there must be sufficient and widespread demand for the services being offered (Montagu, 2002). Many curative services meet these criteria, but preventative services, or diseases requiring long-term treatment are more problematic. Nevertheless, it might be possible to adapt this model to tackle a whole range of interventions, where procedures might be standardised, such as cataract operations and diabetes management.

However, franchises will potentially struggle to balance financial sustainability with the need to serve low-income groups, because of the need to charge patients in order to break even. Therefore it is likely some external assistance would be required, either by directly subsidising the franchisee, or by demand-side interventions such as issuing the poor with vouchers.

Performance-based contracting

One of the most widely used ways of engaging with the private sector is for ministries of health to contract private sector operators and NGOs to deliver defined and measurable services to local populations, usually in a specific location and over a specific time period. Contracts are framed with clear and measurable objectives, and dispense rewards based on meeting these criteria. Conversely, if these criteria are not met, the contract can be terminated or not renewed. Because contracts are framed according to pre-specified outputs they incentivise providers to focus on delivering those outputs in the most efficient manner possible. They also encourage decentralised decision making and management, driving innovation and efficiency. In lower-income countries, performance-based contracting has been widely used in a range of contexts, including providing HIV prevention services, primary health care (PHC) services, diagnostic services and managing hospitals.

There is now a good body of evidence about the usefulness of contracting, and many experiments have taken place in lower-income countries. Broadly, the literature indicates that contracting helps to increase access to health services, while improving equity, quality and efficiency. In their comparison of contracting schemes with similar government provision, Loevinsohn and Harding (2005) find that in all six cases, "the contractors were more effective than the government, on the basis of several measures related to both quality of care and coverage of services". In a number of countries, including Bangladesh, Guatemala, Haiti, India, Bolivia, Madagascar, and Senegal, contracting with non-governmental entities resulted in "rapid improvements". The study goes on to state that contracting is frequently cheaper than government provision, and can increase coverage in poor, remote areas, especially when the contractor is given resources and a specific mandate. As such, contracting is especially useful for increasing access to medicines for the under-served poor, who suffer from the fact that much government-provided nominally "free" healthcare is consumed by wealthier segments of society.

For companies and NGOs, there are several motivations for bidding for these contracts. These include the opportunity to increase revenue, enhance recognition, and increase brand credibility. Evidence from the Middle East suggests governments have established these relationships in order to decentralise management, increase quality, take advantage of economies of scale in the private sector and decrease waiting lists at public hospitals (Sameen, Siddiqi et al; 2006).

One example of where contracting has been widely used is Cambodia, where NGOs have competed to provide health services to the rural poor since 1999. Following the Khmer Rouge's systematic extermination of the educated classes - including doctors - and the subsequent twenty years of fractured governance and civil war, the health care system was in a parlous state. In 1999, the Cambodian Ministry of Health launched an innovative pilot scheme that allowed a direct comparison of different modes of health provision among twelve districts.

Two districts granted complete autonomy for health service provision to NGOs, three districts contracted in NGOs to work within the government system, the government retained control of providing health services in four districts, and the remaining three districts were not formally included in the experiment to serve as a comparison group to the other nine. The NGOs were selected through a competitive bidding process based on the quality of proposals and cost.

A final survey of the results of this experiment was conducted by the World Bank in 2003, which found that, "with only one exception... the contracted districts achieved larger increases in coverage rates than the government districts" and immunisation coverage increased by nearly 60 per cent in the contracted-out districts (World Bank, 2007)[2]. Subsequent independent assessments showed provision became more equal and the quality of care rose most in contracted districts compared to the state-provided districts. Coverage and standards improved so rapidly that the government has since expanded the program to cover one in ten Cambodians. Cambodia is notable for its use of an innovative local financing model, Health Equity Funds, in order to ensure the poorest are able to take advantage of health services. These are discussed in the next section.

Contracting faces some risks, such as: a reliance on donor funds; limited numbers of providers in rural areas; parties with vested interests gaining control over the contracting process; as well as poor monitoring and evaluation mechanisms. However, many of these shortcomings are also faced by the public sector, particularly when it is financed according to input measures. The evidence shows that when appropriate controls are in place, contracting can improve overall health system performance.

Public private partnerships (PPPs)

Many partnerships have been established between the private and public sectors, which take advantage of each other's capabilities and resources. These partnerships take many guises, and span the entire range of services from primary care to advanced diagnostic services. India has seen many PPPs emerge for primary care, and they operate in at least 13 states, and are becoming an increasingly important method of delivering healthcare to the poor, given the constraints faced by the public sector (Pal & Pal, 2009). By harnessing the best features of the private sector, these partnerships can also ensure some degree of accountability. Health PPPs in India are discussed in more detail in Debashis Chakraborty's chapter.

Private sector health delivery - demand side approaches

Microfinance

Although the private sector is the first (and frequently the only port) of call for many people seeking healthcare in low-income countries, many practitioners lack the capital to invest in and expand their clinics and capabilities. Poorly defined property rights and weak contract law make it difficult for such small businesses to secure the loans necessary for expansion. As a result, many small private practitioners such as midwives or physicians are under-equipped and lack the business skills needed to make their practices more viable.

Microfinance, or small loans, has been suggested as a way of building the capacity of the private health sector, and potentially enabling it to tap into more formal arrangements such as franchising. This would increase the capacity and quality of services, helping lower-income countries achieve the goal of providing high quality universal healthcare.

First developed by the Grameen Bank in Bangladesh, the basic micro-credit model of extending loans to impoverished individuals has been widely used by NGOs and local charities in a wide range of sectors from agriculture to water provision. Relatively little is known about the use of microfinance in the health sector, although a handful of studies exist examining the role of microfinance in helping midwives and small private clinics in Africa.

The first study to examine the impact of microfinance on small-scale private health providers (Agha et al, 2004) used client perceptions as a proxy for quality of the service provided by 15 midwives in Uganda who had received microloans. The authors found that the programme had positive effects on client perceptions of the availability of drugs, fair charges, cleanliness and privacy. Midwives reported that the loans allowed them to obtain a bulk discount for medicines, and were able to pass the savings onto clients. The programme had an excellent repayment rate, and midwives were very keen to continue participating in the scheme.

Another study of micro-financed clinics in Uganda found equally encouraging results in the delivery of curative and preventative health services (Seiber & Robinson, 2007). The study found the perceived quality of care improved, with loan recipients' clients being more likely to choose their clinics on the basis of better drug availability, fairer charges, cleanliness, and confidentiality. In addition, the assessment found evidence of increased client flows. In particular, the clinics in question became established as reliable retailers of pharmaceuticals, although questions remain about the clinics rational prescription of medicines.

With regards to HIV, there is no immediately available evidence on micro-financed treatment, although there are numerous prevention projects funded in this manner, as well as insurance against the economic effects of a close relative dying of AIDS.

Community health insurance

Many people in sub Saharan Africa and other poor regions lack access to either public health facilities or coverage by formal private health insurance. Community Health Insurance is one way of providing coverage to the poor, who often work in the informal sector and therefore cannot access formal insurance. These community schemes are generally small-scale, voluntary and non-profit mutual funds, which allow groups of individuals to pool risk more effectively, providing protection against the financial repercussions of illness.

There is now a great deal of evidence to show that community health insurance has the potential to promote access to care, and there are several successful schemes in operation in Africa, such as the Bwamanda Insurance Plan in the DRC, the Nkoranza scheme in Ghana and the government-supported schemes in Rwanda. However, many studies show extremely low rates of enrolment of less than 10 per cent of the target population (Ekman, 2004). Other problems include a fluctuating membership, which makes it impossible to calculate future premiums in an actuarially fair manner (Tabor, 2005), and far higher rates of enrolment by the wealthiest instead of the poor (De Allegri et al, 2006). These low enrolment rates limit the size of the pool and thereby undermine the ability of the fund managers to equalise risk and take advantage of economies of scale.

There are many reasons why Community Health Insurance is not living up to its potential, including a lack of managerial capacity and professional staff; fraud; difficulty in overcoming adverse selection; and high overhead costs compared to the small sizes of risk pools (de Allegri et al, 2009). Also, governments of lower-income countries have failed to foster an institutional environment conducive to the formation of community health insurance, such as presiding over clear legislation and simple regulation.

Because of the low take-up rates of Community Health Insurance, pools are currently of insufficient size to finance treatments for expensive, long-term conditions such as diabetes. If they are to be of use in the longer-term fight against chronic diseases, their overheads will have to be reduced and any regulatory or legislative barriers to their formation will have to be addressed.

Private health insurance

Private health insurance does not have a wide uptake in sub Saharan Africa, partly because of hostile regulatory environments and weak rule of law (which make contracts difficult to uphold). However, private insurance is widespread in South Africa where HIV is highly prevalent, and the government has made antiretroviral drug (ARV) coverage mandatory for all polices. Such mandates, however, make it difficult to balance risk with affordable premiums. Several experiments are underway to spread this risk more widely and thereby reduce the cost to insurers (which in theory could be passed on to consumers). One such experiment comes from Namibia, where insurers pay a subscription to cover the cost of customers who require HIV treatment into a Risk Equalisation Fund (Feeley, 2007). This is a similar principle to the Risk Equalization Fund that underpins the compulsory health insurance system of the Netherlands, which allows coverage to be extended to both the indigent and those with chronic, long-term conditions that might otherwise be an unsustainable drain on insurers.

Health Equity funds

In many poor countries, governments have attempted to cut costs and increase the financial sustainability of public healthcare services by charging user fees. Such user fees, however, frequently deter the poorest from seeking treatment, (even though they can discourage frivolous use of healthcare resources and incentivize compliance). As a way of avoiding user fees, certain countries have established "Health Equity Funds" which raise and manage funds, and pay providers, on behalf of the poorest patients. Many of these funds are privately managed and financed.

Although it has been tried, simply issuing fee exemptions to the poorest has not proved successful, largely because large numbers of non-paying patients can rapidly result in losses for hospitals (Stierle et al, 1999). This loss of income can drive health practitioners to seek other ways to supplement their salaries, such as by selling drugs into the black market or charging informal fees (Ensor, 2004), hurting the poor even more. Meanwhile, user-fees in themselves are not the only barrier to access to quality healthcare: patients are also deterred by the costs of transport, loss of daily income and a lack of knowledge.

Health Equity Funds have been suggested as a way of maintaining the user fees necessary to allow health facilities to operate in a sustainable manner, while ensuring that the poorest can afford those fees, as well as the other costs associated with seeking treatment, such as transport. Generally, the role of the Health Equity Fund is to determine which citizens are eligible to become members, attract and manage financing on their behalf, and then ensure the provider is paid according to the services delivered to its members. The Fund also ensures that participation costs (such as transport) are met. Crucially, Funds are financially and managerially separate to health providers, so it can use its weight as a major customer to ensure the provider adheres to certain standards.

The use of HEFs in the financing of primary care, particularly in Cambodia, is illuminating. Following the rebuilding of the country's health infrastructure following the civil war, the government became concerned about the impact of user fees on the poor, and the inability of waivers to target effectively those most in need. In response, in 2000 the humanitarian NGO Médecins Sans Frontières established a Health Equity fund for the district hospital it supported. Initial results were encouraging; with over 40 per cent of patients at Sotnikum district hospital belonging to the most deprived social group. This caught the eye of local policy makers and donors, who then encouraged the expansion of HEFs throughout the country. By 2006, there were HEFs operational at 26 hospitals or health districts in Cambodia, all of which were managed independently of the Ministry of Health.

As Cambodia's experience demonstrates, HEFs have clearly been successful in increasing access to health services for the poor, often at a low cost. HEFs also work particularly well when used in combination with complementary supply-side initiatives like contracting, which is widespread in Cambodia (Annear *et al.* 2008). However, all of the HEFs with the exception of one have required substantial and ongoing donor or governmental support, which may limit their ability to be rolled out on a large scale. They also rely on the continuing administrative stability of the managing NGO.

Discussion - harnessing the capacity of the private sector in the face of epidemiological shifts

As populations age and become wealthier, infectious diseases are rapidly being replaced by Non Communicable Diseases such a cancer and diabetes as the largest problem faced by health systems. Public healthcare systems in middle and lower-income countries are struggling with their current workload, and look badly placed to handle this epidemiological shift. Fortunately, there is a great deal of capacity within the private sector to shoulder some of this burden, but the question of how to involve them in the most equitable way has yet to be fully resolved.

1. Franchising can help assure quality in healthcare provision

Although the private sector is very often the main provider of healthcare in low and middle income countries, its quality can be highly variable. Social franchising is one way of improving the quality of private provision, which would benefit the poor in particular. The high start-up costs faced by a franchise may mean that they require external subsidy, either from government or overseas donors. Franchises will only be financially sustainable if they offer a wide range of services, which makes them appropriate for the provision of primary care. Additionally, the quality and availability of many more advanced services, such as diagnostics and simple surgical treatments like cataract removal could be improved by this model - not least because franchises can take advantages of economies of scale to drive down procurement, training and operational costs.

2. Contracting can reduce costs and promote access

The franchise model requires paying customers if it is to be sustainable, which raises the question of how it might benefit the poor. Experiments with contracting private organisations to provide healthcare to lower-income groups are particularly promising in this regard, and could feasibly be combined with franchising in order to expand access. Its particular advantage is that it can be geographically or socially targeted, with payment contingent on actually delivering results. This gives providers a genuine financial incentive to deliver healthcare to the poor, in contrast to traditional public sector provision, which is typically subsidised up-front according to staffing levels or similar arbitrary input measures. Many of the most successful contracting schemes have operated with minimal managerial oversight from the commissioning government ministry, which has provided room for managerial experimentation and innovation.

Most contracting schemes to date, however, have focused on the delivery of primary care, which is clearly measurable in terms of vaccinations dispensed etc. Specialist in-patient care for non-communicable diseases presents greater problems for this model as it is much more difficult to measure performance. For more routine outpatient interventions, though, this model is promising, especially when combined with demand-side financing models that subsidise the poor.

3. Health Equity Funds show promise

There has been a great deal of experimentation with demand-side financing, much of it targeted directly at the poor. Health Equity Funds have demonstrated themselves as indispensible for increasing access for the indigent and poorest, although the majority have required large levels of on-going financial support from government. However, there are examples of self-sustaining HEFs which work at the grass roots through local religious institutions both to raise funds and administer the scheme. Much of this success has been due to its financial and managerial autonomy from government, so this model should be explored more thoroughly.

4. Barriers to health insurance should be reduced

Similarly, private risk pooling schemes have potential to remove the financing burden from the public purse, as well as ensure patients do not have to pay out of pocket for healthcare. However, community health insurance is currently underused, and has been hampered by overly bureaucratic regulations and unclear and uncertain legislative environments. Private health insurance is also not widely available in lower-income countries for similar reasons, even though there are several examples of insurers providing cover for the indigent and high-risk diseases such as HIV. Governments should aim to remove bureaucratic barriers to the formation of private risk pools, and perhaps encourage the formation of new schemes by granting tax breaks.

5. Public Private Partnerships can inject expertise and resources

Public healthcare systems in poor countries often lack the skills and capital to deliver complex care. Public private partnerships are one way of bridging those gaps, as can be seen from examples such as the Botswana ACHAP partnership between the government, Merck and the Gates Foundation. The numbers of global health public private partnerships have increased hugely since the mid 1990s, although there have been complaints that they disrupt and fragment local public health systems, and should therefore be subject to a global framework of rules and norms administered by the UN (Nishtar, 2004). Nevertheless, many public sectors are already fragmented and lacking in suitably qualified staff, so governments should not erect unnecessary bureaucratic barriers to these injections of private skill and capacity. Such PPPs will become even more indispensible in transferring skills and technology to developing countries attempting to tackle NCDs. However, public private partnerships are only as sustainable as the businesses behind them, so should only ever be a complement to, rather than replacement for proper risk pooling arrangements and other forms of self-financing.

Concluding remarks

Above all, the experience of private sector healthcare delivery in lower and middle- income countries - particularly contracting - highlights the ability of operators to innovate and experiment in order to bring costs down while expanding services. Increasing capacity as cheaply as possible will be essential if the goal of Universal Health Coverage is to be achieved. Although governments have a role to play commissioning services, setting standards and monitoring quality, it is essential that providers be given the managerial autonomy necessary to function competitively. Governments should also take steps to remove barriers to the formation of private risk pools and new health providers.

For governments, the biggest lesson is to move away from the kind of state-centric approaches favoured by the World Health Organization, in which "healthcare for all" can only be delivered by public provision of services. As this chapter shows, exciting results can be achieved when governments embrace a plurality of providers, and experiment with incentive-based delivery models. As populations' age and non-communicable diseases become more prevalent in lower and middle-income countries, these models will provide the flexibility and innovative capacity required to genuinely achieve universal healthcare.

Notes

1. Available at http://planningcommission.nic.in/reports/genrep/rep_uhc0812.pdf
2. Available at http://siteresources.worldbank.org/INTPAH/Resources/Reaching-the-Poor/RPPBriefsCambodiaREV.pdf

Bibliography

Agha, S; Balal, A; Ogojo-Okello, F. (2004), "The Impact of a Microfinance Program on Client Perceptions of the Quality of Care Provided by Private Sector Midwives in Uganda", *Health Service Research,* 39(6-2): 2081-2100.

Annear, P et al. (2008), "Providing Access to Health Services for the Poor: Health Equity in Cambodia", *Studies in Health Services Organisation & Policy,* 23: 189-225.

Black, R et al. (2009), "Accelerating the health impact of the Gates Foundation," *The Lancet* 373(9675): 1584-1585.

Chokshi, D. (2006), "Improving Access to Medicines in Poor Countries: The Role of Universities," *PLoS Medicine*, 3(6): e136.

De Allegri, M et al. (2009), "Community health insurance in sub-Saharan Africa: what operational difficulties hamper its successful development?" *Tropical Medicine & International Health* 14(5): 586-596.

De Costa, A and Diwan, V. (2007), "Where is the public health sector? Public and private sector healthcare provision in Madhya Pradesh, India." *Health Policy*, 84(2-3): 269-276.

Eichler, R; Glassman, A. (2008), "Health Systems Strengthening Via Performance-Based Aid: Creating Incentives to Perform and to Measure Results," Global Health Financing Initiative Working Paper 3. Washington, DC: Brookings Institute.

Ekman, B. (2004), "Community-based health insurance in low-income countries: a systematic review of the evidence." *Health Policy and Planning*, 19(5): 249–270.

England, R. (2006), "HIV Antiretroviral Therapy: Can Franchising Expand Coverage?" London: DFID Health Resource Centre, available at http://www.dfidhealthrc.org/publications/health_service_delivery/ART%20and%20social%20franchising_Oct%2006.pdf

Ensor, T. (2004), "Informal payments for health care in transition economies." *Social Science & Medicine*, 58(2): 237–246.

Feeley, F; Connelly, P; Rosen, S. (2007), "Private Sector Provision and Financing of AIDS Treatment in Africa: Current Developments", *Current HIV/AIDS Reports* 4(4): 192–200.

Hanson, K. & P. Berman (1998), "Private health care provision in developing countries: a preliminary analysis of levels and composition." *Health Policy Plan*, 13(3): 195-211.

Hardeman, W et al. (2004), "Access to health care for all? User fees plus a Health Equity Fund in Sotnikum, Cambodia", *Health Policy and Planning*, 19 (1): 22-32.

International Finance Corporation (2007), "The business of health in Africa. World Bank Group." available at: http://www.ifc.org/ifcext/healthinafrica .nsf/Content/FullReport,

Jacobs, B and Price, N. (2003), "Community participation in externally funded health projects: lessons from Cambodia." *Health Policy and Planning*, 18(4): 399–410.

Jacobs, B; Price, N; Sam, O. (2007), "A sustainability assessment of a health equity fund initiative in Cambodia," *The International Journal of Health Planning and Management*, 22(3): 183-203.

Khan, Iram A. (2009), "Public sector institutions, politics and outsourcing: Reforming the provision of primary healthcare in Punjab, Pakistan," *Journal of International Development*, 22(4): 424-440.

Leppert, G. (2010), "Micro health insurance in developing countries: What are the solutions to insurance-related weaknesses of the mutual model?" Unpublished paper. available at http://www.agi-genoforschung.de/files/leppert-2010_micro-health-insurance-in-developing-countrie.pdf

Lewis, M. (2006), "Governance and Corruption in Public Health Care Systems." Center for Global Development, [Internet], Working Paper no. 78.

Liu, X.; Hotchkiss, D.; Bose; S. (2007), "The impact of contracting-out on health system performance: A conceptual framework," *Health Policy*, 82(2): 200-211.

Loevinsohn, B., & Harding. A. (2005), "Buying results? Contracting for health service delivery in developing countries", *The Lancet*; 366: 676–81.

McCoy, D. et al. (2009), "The Bill & Melinda Gates Foundation's grant-making programme for global health," *The Lancet* 373(9675): 1645-1653.

Meessen, B. et al. (2006), "Reviewing institutions of rural health centres: the Performance Initiative in Butare, Rwanda", *Tropical Medicine and International Health*, 11(8): 1303-1317.

Montagu, D. (2002), "Franchising of Health Services in Low-Income Countries", *Health Policy and Planning*, 17(2): 121–130.

Murray, C. et al. (2010), "Public financing of health in developing countries: a cross-national systematic examination." *Lancet* 375(9723): 1375-1387.

Nishtar, S. (2004), "Public-private partnerships in health - a global call to action." *Health Research Policy Systems*, [Internet], Available at: http://www.health-policy-systems.com/content/2/1/5,

Noirhomme, M. et al. (2007), "Improving Access to Hospital Care for the Poor: Comparative Analysis of Four Health Equity Funds in Cambodia", *Health Policy and Planning*, 22(4): 246-262.

Pal & Pal, (2009), "Primary health care and public-private partnership: an Indian perspective", *Annals of Tropical Medicine and Public Health*, 2:2.

Powell-Jackson, T and Mills, A. (2007), "A review of health resource tracking in developing countries." *Health Policy Plan*, 22(6): 353-62.

Pratal, N; Montagu, D; Jefferys, E. (2005), "Private sector, human resources and health franchising in Africa", *Bulletin of the World Health Organisation*, 83(4).

Pritchett, L and Filmer D. (1999), "The Impact of Public Spending on Health: Does Money Matter?" *Social Science and Medicine*, 49(10): 1309-1323.

Ramiah, I; Reich, M. (2005), "Public-Private Partnerships and Antiretroviral Drugs for HIV/AIDS: Lessons from Botswana," *Health Affairs*, 24(2): 545-551.

Rockefeller Foundation (2008), "The role of the private sector in health systems." New York: Rockefeller Foundation.

Schieber, G et al. (2007), "Financing Global Health: Mission Unaccomplished," *Health Affairs*, 26 (4): 921-934.

Schwartz, J., & Bhushan, I. (2005), "Cambodia: using contracting to reduce inequity in primary health care delivery" in *Reaching the Poor with health, nutrition and population services*, World Bank.

Seiber, E and Robinson, A. (2007), "Microfinance investments in quality at private clinics in Uganda: a case-control study", *BMC Health Services Research*, 7(168).

Siddiqi, S et al. (2006), "Contracting but not without caution: experience with outsourcing of health services in countries of the Eastern Mediterranean Region," *Bulletin of the World Health Organization*, 84(11).

Soeters, R; Habineza, C; Peerenboom, P. (2006), "Performance-based financing and changing the district health system: experience from Rwanda," *Bulletin of the World Health Organization*, 84(11).

Stierle, F. (1999), "Indigence and access to health care in sub-Saharan Africa." *International Journal of Health Planning and Management*, 14(2): 81-105.

Tabor, S. (2005), "Community-Based Health Insurance and Social Protection Policy." Social Protection Discussion Paper Series No 0503. Social Protection Unit, Human Development Network, The World Bank, [Internet], Available at: http://tric.ru/files/2006/01/18/CD-Rom%20Content/pdfs/Papers/English/0503.pdf.

Transparency International (2006), "Global Corruption Report: Special focus, Corruption in Healthcare", Berlin.

7

HEALTH VOUCHERS: EXPANDING ACCESS TO HEALTHCARE SERVICES IN PAKISTAN

Mehreen Zahid Malik & Ali Salman[1]

Access to quality healthcare for low-income groups has remained a priority for governments and donors working in developing countries alike. In spite of increased efforts by governments, donors, civil society (local, national and international NGOs and community based organisations) and bilateral and multilateral organisations, access to at least a basic but high impact health services package and education by low income groups is still beyond the reach of millions.

Healthcare in Pakistan has undergone many changes over the last thirty years, moving from a largely curative approach to one based more on primary health care (i.e. focus on prevention), following the signing of the Alma-Ata Declaration in 1978[2] (Shaikh and Kadir et al, 2007). More recently, in line with the Millennium Development Goals (MDGs), there has been an increased focus on health, especially maternal and child health. Draft National Health Policy of Pakistan 2009 (Government of Pakistan, 2009) envisions 'health for all' while calling for health sector reforms to realize this vision.

Although a wide range of services are available to the general public there is still a gap to be filled especially with regard to the accessibility of health services for low-income groups such as labourers, minorities, domestic workers, and street vendors. Barriers to health access include low-income levels, lack of awareness about services, geographical inaccessibility, and the attitude of the healthcare providers.

Also according to the draft of the Health Policy on Pakistan, the total expenditure on health is about 2 percent of GDP, much lower than in other countries with similar income levels. A third of this expenditure is contributed by the government and 70 per cent is paid out-of-pocket by the citizens at the point of service delivery (Government of Pakistan, 2009).

Public support policies in developing countries focus on public financing and provision, usually through supply-side subsidies such as subsidised or 'free at the point of use' public health services, so as to ensure access to healthcare for all. On the demand side, delivery strategies such as Health Vouchers have been introduced. Demand-side strategies improve access through empowering the users of healthcare who 'vote with their feet', forcing providers to be responsive and innovative.

This chapter reviews international practices in provision of health vouchers in order to determine how they might be adapted to Pakistan. It was conducted as part of a project by the Alternate Solutions Institute, a Pakistan-based think tank that aims to explore innovative, non-state solutions to healthcare problems faced by Pakistanis. The review of international best practices shows that in general there is a focus on maternal health, reproductive health or sexually transmitted infections (STIs). Contextualizing/ adapting these international practices to Pakistan is needed and an amalgamation of these different schemes can be used to design a new product in Pakistan.

Supply-side approaches to expand access to healthcare

Most governments of developing countries seek to improve healthcare by attempting to improve the supply of healthcare. As a result, the most common methods of health reform include public subsidies, increasing performance accountability, and leveraging public resources with private participation and financing, i.e. public-private partnerships.

Many of these supply-side measures come with a large price tag. In order to meet the burden of the supply-side subsidy, governments struggle to meet the costs of increasing public expectations for free health services. Vast sums are wasted on ineffective interventions while the health systems themselves are also full of administrative and technical inefficiencies. This results in inaccessibility of health services for the intended beneficiaries, namely the poor and the vulnerable (World Bank, 2004), including women and children.

Demand-side Approaches to improve access to healthcare

To further overcome problems of access to healthcare services, policymakers have tried several demand-side approaches to finance healthcare through subsidising the consumer of healthcare directly (USAID, 2007). These approaches to healthcare access include:

- Behavioural change to influence health outcomes - including education on a healthier lifestyle, and the improvements brought by changes in behaviour.
- Rights-based approaches, which promote healthcare access as a basic human right.
- Participatory approaches - consultations with users on resource allocation, mobilization of resources, oversight and monitoring of services and providers, and civil society based initiatives in markets.

- Multi-sectored/multiple stakeholder approaches - include the government sector and the social sector, the civil society, and their target communities.
- Demand-side financing - give either financial or other kinds of transfers through a third party payment, directly to a client/user.

Source: DfID, 2004

This chapter focuses on this last strategy of demand-side financing by looking at health vouchers, in which patients are given funding to take to a healthcare provider of their choice. Schemes such as health vouchers have been found to be successful for providing access to health services for low-income groups (DfID, 2004). Voucher schemes can increase equity in access to specified health services, because they remove cost and quality barriers to service uptake and because it is possible to target their distribution to disadvantaged groups (ICAS, 2003).

Health Vouchers

Vouchers are targeted at identified groups (such as the low income group), they are exchanged for specific services and they are usually aimed at providing access in the private sector as public care is either free or low-cost. Also the level of financing available in the voucher scheme depends on the services and products. Thus, it may be provided free of charge or at a reduced price by providers / stakeholders / partners participating in the voucher programme. Voucher programmes enable low-income patients to make use of good quality healthcare and health services, at reduced rates and per unit costs (Population Council).

Review of international best practices

This section reviews some international best practices from around the world. The purpose for reviewing these is twofold; to learn from best international practices and use this insight to develop policy framework for a new health voucher scheme in Pakistan. Models included are:

1. Chiranjeevi Yojana
2. Reproductive Health Voucher Programme Kenya
3. Bangladesh maternal voucher scheme
4. ICAS, Nicaragua
5. Uganda voucher
6. Taiwan health voucher

Chiranjeevi Scheme (India)

The Chiranjeevi Yojana ("eternal life scheme") was an output-based aid (OBA) voucher programme for reproductive health services which started in Gujarat, India in 2005. Its objective was to improve infant and maternal mortality rates by providing access in the private sector for those pregnant women that lived below the poverty line. The scheme was launched as a one-year pilot project in five districts: Banaskantha, Dahod, Kutch, Panchmahal, and Sabarkantha. The scheme has now been extended to the entire state (Bhat et. al, 2009).

This voucher scheme provided a transport stipend after which the private providers (partners in the scheme) were reimbursed on a per head payment basis that was fixed. These partners were identified by the Block Health Officer (BHO).

The payments of the vouchers were made for a batch of 100 childbirths that were a mixture of normal as well as complicated deliveries. An average cost per delivery was worked out using the market rates for a normal and a complicated delivery; this was then used as per head cost.

Services provided through the vouchers were:

- Antenatal care
- Postnatal care
- Transportation costs
- Delivery

Reproductive Health Output-Based Aid Voucher Programme Kenya[3]:

This voucher scheme, which was operational between 2005 and 2012, was funded by the KFW German Development Bank and the Kenyan government. It comprises two phases:

1. Phase I from October 2005 to October 2008
2. Phase II from June 2009 to 2012

The scheme provides a safe motherhood package of antenatal services and attended delivery by qualified health workers, long-term family planning methods and gender-based violence recovery services at ascribed facilities. The service providers in this project were selected on the basis of their capacity to provide the previously mentioned set of services against this voucher scheme and they included both public and private practitioners.

The cost is fixed at dollar rates for all the services as follows:

- The safe motherhood voucher cost to clients is $2.70.
- The Family Planning voucher costs $1.35.
- The service providers are reimbursed up to an amount of $276 for complicated deliveries.

Marketing of the scheme was done through advertisements of a one-month campaign that increased awareness about the vouchers. As a result of a participatory poverty grading tool, the districts identified as targets were: Kisumu, Kiambu, and Kitui districts as well as Korogocho and Viwandani slums (Nairobi).

Bangladesh maternal voucher scheme[4]:

In line with achieving the Millennium Development Goals (MDGs), the Government of Bangladesh has initiated a "demand-side financing maternal health voucher scheme" for poor mothers in 21 sub-districts of Bangladesh. This scheme was started in collaboration with the World Bank and WHO, after the following interventions that took place in Bangladesh:

- The Bangladesh Association of Voluntary Sterilisation (BAVS) implemented a home-based Skilled Birth Attendant (SBA) programme between 1992 and 1997 in all rural unions of Chandpur, Sadar, Upazila about 60 km south and south-east of Dhaka. These SBAs were trained in midwifery including hands-on birthing experience to do safe home-deliveries and provide antenatal and postnatal care services in their respective communities.
- The Non-governmental Organization (NGO) Service Delivery Project (NSDP), in collaboration with its partner NGOs initiated a home-based SBA programme in 10 different rural and peri-urban areas of the country with its existing nurses or midwives in May 2005.
- In February to May 2006, the International Centre for Diarrhoeal Disease, Bangladesh (ICDDR, B) evaluated these two home-based SBA programmes for their functionality, use and sustainability.

These programmes helped lay the groundwork for the health voucher scheme in Bangladesh. The targeted women for this scheme were identified by local committees on the basis of a set criteria, and hence the women were provided with vouchers to buy maternal health-care services (including treatment for obstetric complications) from different preselected providers (public and private) or facilities already in the area.

ICAS, Nicaragua[5]:

The Central American Health Institute (ICAS) is a non-governmental organisation based in Nicaragua and devoted to improving the quality of life of the population including the poorest and most vulnerable groups. It has over 16 years of experience in support of the health and rights of Nicaragua's most vulnerable groups especially adolescents and young people, drug addicts, sex workers and their partners and clients, homosexual men, prisoners, mobile populations, poor rural women and other groups with insufficient access to social and health services and information.

Since 1995 ICAS has run a competitive voucher programme promoting the rights of vulnerable groups through their voucher scheme while also being involved in spreading awareness through education, lobbying and advocacy. It is one of the world's first voucher schemes for health services that has helped provide identified vulnerable groups with access to prescribed health services.

The vouchers used to increase access are:

- For adolescents from 2000 to 2005 – sexual and reproductive health services.
- For population at high risk for HIV from 1995 to present – STI/HIV/AIDS services.
- For older poor rural women from 1998 onwards – breast and cervical cancer screening.

The voucher scheme began as a research programme providing free-of-charge prevention and treatment services for STIs in Managua. The voucher programme now also includes Voluntary Counseling and Testing for HIV and follow-up and care of people living with HIV/AIDS, including pregnant women.

Uganda voucher[6]:

This programme was launched in July 2006 where more than 19,000 patients were looked at for complaints of sexually transmitted infections (STIs). It was started by the following organizations:

- Marie Stopes International Uganda
- Venture strategies for health and development
- Mbarara University of Science and Technology, Department of Community Health (DOCH)
- KFW development bank
- Uganda Ministry of Health
- Microcare Limited

Along with STI treatments the voucher offers use of low-cost lab technologies (wet mount and a microscope) and partner referral. A financial contract with partner providers ensures that there is a means to check compliance with quality lab and management standards.

Taiwan health voucher[7]:

The Taiwan Ministry of Health offered male and female sterilization services at a range of government and private facilities. These were provided through an OBA voucher scheme to low income couples, and this voucher provided a subsidy on a routine health service to those couples that participated in sterilization.

The voucher targeted couples with two or more children. Couples who did not qualify for the voucher could buy their vouchers and visit their selected provider. Thus they did not pay the fee but received the same voucher chosen from the same network of providers and received the same level of care.

Analysis of International Practices

The review of international best practices above shows that in general there is a focus on either maternal health or reproductive health. Maternal health is focused on in India, Kenya and Bangladesh, while other voucher schemes such as ICAS, Taiwan, and Uganda focus on the reproductive health.

This Chiranjeevi scheme's most important aspect was the transport stipend that it provided for the users of the voucher scheme. A further point to note is the price of the voucher, which was calculated as an average of the market rates of a normal and a complicated delivery. This element of the Chiranjeevi scheme can also be tested in Pakistan. In fact this model for maternal health schemes can be replicated as a whole for the low-income group of Pakistan identified later.

The Reproductive Health voucher scheme in Kenya emphasizes the same services as the Indian scheme with an important difference; the scheme created awareness through a month-long advertising campaign. This awareness for a voucher scheme should be an integral part of any health voucher proposal. Again such a scheme can well be implemented in Pakistan with the price of voucher calculated either according to the needs of the target group and donor budget or via an average similar to Chiranjeevi scheme.

The ICAS scheme is a fully implementable scheme in and of itself. However, a major point to note here is that subjects such as STI/HIV/AIDS were previously taboo and have only recently starting seeing greater discussion and work in Pakistan's health sector.

Other issues related to sexual and reproductive health, their education and prevention have been in place at governmental organisations for some time. The breast and cervical screening part of this scheme along with its counseling and follow up visits should also be implemented in Pakistan.

As stated for the Kenya scheme, there is also a need for awareness of the scheme being implemented before the vouchers have been distributed. The Uganda voucher scheme is similar to ICAS and this too is related to STIs. While ICAS targets a significant proportion of the population and a wide variety of diseases the Uganda voucher deals with just STI complaints. An important point in this scheme is the public-private partnership being pursued to implement the STI treatment voucher project. There is also an emphasis on the monitoring of the scheme showing that it should be an integral part of any health voucher scheme.

The Taiwanese example is unique in that it provides a subsidy on any routine health service if the participants are involved in sterilization. This type of scheme can also be replicated in a Pakistani context. Although sterilization is not part of the agenda in Pakistan, this sort of a voucher can act as an incentive for low-income groups to pursue the sterilization process, as having a large number of children is indeed a problem that Pakistan faces. Contextualizing these international practices to Pakistan is needed and an amalgamation of these different schemes can lead to a unique and indigenous product in Pakistan.

Lessons Learned from International Practices for Pakistan

- To ensure that the recipients of health vouchers actually benefit from it, a transport stipend may be added in areas where mobility is a problem.
- In pricing a voucher, market based services should be taken as a benchmark.
- Many voucher schemes fail simply because the target beneficiaries do not know about them, therefore a promotional and awareness campaign should be launched.
- The health vouchers may accord some preferences to more prevalent diseases or health related problems pertaining to specific location.
- Providing health vouchers to needy patients may be conditioned with some desirable healthcare practice or behaviour such as in the case of family planning.

Policy Proposal

The voucher should target the disadvantaged population to increase access to health services and also increase the utilisation of these services. This can also effectively be used to improve the quality of services through an increase in competition. Finally, the recommended mode for setting up a successful and effective voucher is a partnership between the public, private and NGO sectors.

Before designing the health voucher scheme, the following considerations and factors must be taken into account.

- Identifying priority package of health services to be provided
- Cost and cost-effectiveness
- Pricing of the voucher
- Distribution
- Characteristics

- Monitoring and evaluating a voucher programme
- Risks, misuse, and remedial strategies

Cost Implications for implementation:

A few considerations for determining the cost for any donor to look into while implementing a health voucher scheme are as follows (World Bank, 2004):

- The redemption value of the vouchers
- The value for the voucher agency
- The logistics required to run the scheme
- The marketing costs
- The distribution costs
- The training costs
- The production cost of the vouchers
- Monitoring and audit

The best way to efficiently find the cost of the voucher scheme and estimate a rate for the voucher, and its potential benefits and obstacles is to perform a pilot test before the actual implementation of the scheme.

Pricing of the voucher

Pricing a voucher can be difficult in a situation such as the one described above where one end of the continuum includes claimed free services by the government and on the other there are extremely expensive testing/diagnostic services and operations. The list of feasible options available include: making the voucher fully paid for all services offered, or giving all the services at half the rate of the original price of the services that the voucher is redeemed against. The pricing eventually will depend on the donor assistance and the specific area targeted.

The following table taken from the World Bank report accurately aligns with our needs of healthcare access to the low-income group as it covers the wide range of services that are desirable.

Table 1: Menu of Services Required under Healthcare Access

Provision of Medicines	*Consultation Counseling Services*	*Diagnostic/ testing services*	*Operations*	*Monetary Assistance*
Pain medication	Maternal and infant health	Ultra sound	Delivery	Zakat
Antacids	STI/HIV/AIDS education	X-ray	Appendix	Bait-ul-maal
STI medicine	General Consultations	ECG	Tumor removal	Micro-insurance
Hepatitis C medicine		CT-scan	Gal bladder operation	Vouchers
T.B. medication		MRI		

Source: World Bank (2004)

Distribution

An important aspect of the health voucher scheme concerns the distribution of the voucher to its intended users, in this case the low-income groups comprising of:

1. Labourers
2. Domestic workers
3. Minorities
4. Street Vendors
5. Other marginalized segments

The distribution will also depend on the funding level of the voucher scheme. The vouchers can be distributed by either the organisation that has designed the voucher, by an external agency that has been contracted by the voucher agency, or they could be given directly to the beneficiaries. If the vouchers are to be distributed directly to the beneficiaries (i.e. the low income group) then the voucher agency can do it through various dispensing points. Here the users can pick up the vouchers themselves thus further lowering costs for the funding organisation (The World Bank, 2004). Distribution through local leaders can be beneficial for a donor as the leaders will know who to target, the costs are kept down and the vouchers still reach the intended end users.

Monitoring and evaluating a Voucher Programme

In the case of implementing a voucher scheme, monitoring and evaluation will determine if the scheme is being targeted and utilised correctly, that it is geared towards the right audience, and whether its quality is being maintained.

One of the main concerns with regard to the distribution strategy is incorporating an effective measure of checks and balances to ensure that the vouchers indeed reach targeted users. Thus an effective monitoring system needs to be implemented.

The voucher issuing agency should have the serial numbers on the vouchers recorded as a way to monitor the distribution strategy. Through the serial numbers a check and balance is also provided to prevent the distribution of vouchers at points other than that of service delivery and to prevent the misuse of the vouchers. Another aspect that donor agencies need to be mindful of is the possibility of nepotism at the dispensing point. While it would be difficult to always stop this, one option is to regularly interview low-income groups in the vicinity to track whether the intended users are indeed receiving the vouchers. A community based approach to design and manage health vouchers would ensure that the scheme remains under watch by the community members.

Risks, misuse, and remedial strategies

The risks relating to a voucher scheme include misuse of the voucher at all levels of the scheme, from piloting to implementation. Limitations and the operational shortcomings of the scheme - such as distribution and the utilisation of the voucher - are also a risk (Por I. et al., 2010).

The following risks are identified by the World Bank:

1. **Counterfeiting** – this occurs when a black market for the voucher comes into existence, issuing counterfeit vouchers. It usually occurs for a service that is highly sought after, or if the monetary value for that service is high.

2. **Collusion** – this takes place between the voucher distributor and the healthcare service provider. The voucher distributors may collude with the provider to exchange the voucher for a portion of the earnings.

3. **Black markets** – if the demand for a voucher is high then a black market for the vouchers may develop to make a profit out of the increased demand.

4. **Dishonesty within the voucher agency** – the staff of the voucher agency may be bribed by the providers into contracting with providing them the vouchers or even agreeing to higher payments to the providers.

5. **Over servicing** – also known as the 'moral hazard' in the health insurance schemes, it takes place when providers are tempted to bring in a patient from a high-income group. This is usually done when the voucher agency gives the payments to providers on the basis of patient characteristics.

6. **Adverse selection** – adverse selection happens when the voucher incorporates an element of risk spreading. When the voucher covers both the screening tests and the treatment of a disease then the possibility arises whereby a screened patient (diagnosed elsewhere) will only purchase a voucher to subsidise the cost of treatment if they test positive.

A voucher scheme faces additional risks. Existing providers that are to be involved in the voucher scheme would need to be brought up to the performance level necessary to ensure the quality of the scheme (Por I. et al., 2010). This can be a financial risk for the voucher agency and a constraint for the implementation of the scheme, especially if the budget is low.

Some non-financial constraints to consider are: the distance that a user will have to cover to either redeem or use a voucher; and intra-household constraints of the user or socio-cultural practices (Ibid). If such constraints are widespread then there is a high probability that the voucher scheme will not be successful as such a scenario would mean the end users would fail to even procure the vouchers; the scheme then would not be fulfilling its basic objective of reaching its intended targets.

Most of the risks and the resulting misuse of the voucher schemes can be simply countered by a good monitoring system. As the section on monitoring and evaluation shows, there should be monitoring of everything, from costs to quality to providers etc. Having regular field visits, facility inspections, and some surprise monitoring visits will also prevent misuse of the scheme. The black market risk for the scheme can be overcome by clearly stating on the voucher that it has no monetary value, and in case of counterfeiting, a record of the serial numbers on the vouchers should be kept and be regularly updated.

Finally it should be stressed again that any voucher schemes should be started off with a pilot before scaling up to assess the feasibility of the scheme, identify users of the scheme, and pinpoint the services that can be offered against such a scheme. Quality, reliability and accessibility of the scheme can all be determined.

Conclusion

This chapter outlines a framework for a health voucher policy that can be implemented in Pakistan for increasing access to healthcare services for low- income groups. It describes basic parameters of the model: the cost complications for implementation of a health voucher scheme; the pricing strategy of the voucher; its distribution; its characteristics; monitoring and evaluating effectiveness; and the risks, misuse, and remedial strategies for the health voucher scheme.

Some international best practices of health voucher schemes are also reviewed in the chapter. Several schemes have been successful in reaching low-income groups by providing healthcare services through vouchers that provide subsidies on the provision of certain healthcare services, mostly related to reproductive health and education.

It is noteworthy that there are also examples of several health voucher schemes already in place in Pakistan. Some of these provide vouchers to acquire maternal and child healthcare services, along with RH services and education – the NARI scheme, and MSS vouchers. A private sector approach to health vouchers has been demonstrated by the experience of Medi Card. These practices help in identifying basic contours of health vouchers scheme in Pakistan. It is stressed that any health voucher scheme will be successful if it is implemented with public-private partnerships.

This chapter recommends development of an alternative system of providing healthcare access to low-income groups by comparing different models of health vouchers. The report argues that there is indeed a need for increasing access to healthcare services for the low income groups in Pakistan and that a health voucher will help in this endeavour. Furthermore, the public prefers private healthcare because at the government centres and hospitals, either no one is present or the personnel present are too overworked to attend to all their patients. Hence, the report emphasises this need for alternate financing of and access to healthcare services for the low-income group in a sustainable and market friendly mechanism.

Notes

1. Alternate Solutions Institute, Lahore, Pakistan.
2. Development consultant, policy entrepreneur and economic analyst based in Islamabad, Pakistan.
3. The International Conference on Primary Health Care, meeting in Alma-Ata 1978, expressed the need for urgent action by all governments, all health and development workers, and the world community to protect and promote the health of all the people of the world. The conference resulted in a declaration which called for the national and international actors to develop and implement primary healthcare throughout the

world. Online. Available http://www.who.int/hpr/NPH/docs/declaration_almaata.pdf

4. Based on: http://www.rhvouchers.org/kenya/
5. This section is based on: http://www.who.int/bulletin/volumes/86/4/07-042754/en/
6. Source: http://www.rhvouchers.org/nicaragua/
7. Source: http://www.rhvouchers.org/uganda/
8. Source: http://www.rhvouchers.org/taiwan/

References

Anwar, I, M Sami, N Akhtar, ME Chowdhury, U Salma, M Rahman, M Koblinsky (2008), "Inequity in maternal health-care services: evidence from home-based skilled-birth-attendant programmes in Bangladesh", Bulletin of World Health Organization, available at. http://www.who.int/bulletin/volumes/86/4/07-042754/en/ (accessed June 10, 2010).

Bhat, Ramesh, Dileep V. Mavalankar, Prabal V. Singh, and Neelu Singh (2009), "Maternal Healthcare Financing: Gujarat's Chiranjeevi Scheme and Its Beneficiaries", . *Journal of Health, Population and Nutrition*, 27, (No. 22): 249-258., http://www.bioline.org.br/request?hn09023 (accessed June 12, 2010).

Department for International Development (DfID) (, 2004), ". Understanding the demand side in service delivery – Definitions, frameworks and tools from the health sector", available at 2004.http://www.dfidhealthrc.org/publications/health_service_delivery/Standing.pdf

Government of Pakistan (2009), "National Health Policy, 2009", Islamabad.

Government of Pakistan (2010), "National Rural Support Programme, 2010", Islamabad.

Government of Punjab (undated), "Minimum Service Delivery Standards for Primary and Secondary Health Care in Punjab", available at .http://www.pdssp.gop.pk/downloads/documents/MSDS%20_ Health_ % 20Final.pdf

Instituto Centro Americano de la Salud (ICAS)ICAS (, 2003), "Competitive Voucher Schemes for Health Background Paper", available at .Instituto Centro Americano de la Salud (ICAS). www.icas.net.

Instituto Centro Americano de la Salud (ICAS) (2003), "ICAS, 2003. Programme for the prevention and treatment of STI-HIV-AIDS", available at .http://www.icas.net/new-icasweb/english/en_vih_sida.html

Marie Stopes International (undated), "Fact sheet out-put based aid. Focused on results: How Marie Stopes International (MSI) is pioneering the use of Output-based aid (OBA) to scale-up health services for women", available at .http://www.mariestopes.org/documents/Output-based%20aid.pdf

Marie Stopes Society (undated), "Services", available at http://www.mariestopespk.org/services_Services.asp

Medi Card (undated), "Pakistan's first managed family healthcare card", available at http://www.medicard.org.pk/index.html

Pappas G., A. Ghaffar, T. Masud, A. Hyder, and S. Siddiqi (2009), "Governance and health sector development: a case study of Pakistan", *The Internet Journal of World Health and Societal Politics*, 7(1). http://www.ispub.com/journal/the_internet_ journal_ of_world_health_and_societal_politics/volume_7_number_1_33/article/governance- and-health-sector-development-a-case-study-of-pakistan.html (accessed June 15, 2010).

Population Council (undated), "Evaluating Voucher-and-Accreditation Interventions to Improve Reproductive Health Service Delivery Business Models", available at .http://www.popcouncil.org/projects/231_EvalVouchAccredRH.asp

Por Ir., Dirk Horemans, Narin Souk, and Wim Van Damme (2010), "Using targeted vouchers and health equity funds to improve access to skilled birth attendants for poor women: a case study in three rural health districts in Cambodia", *BioMed Central*, available at http://www.biomedcentral.com/1471-2393/10/1 (last accesseds June 20, 2010).

Shaikh, Baber T., Muhammad Masood Kadir, and Gregory Pappas (2007), "Thirty years of Alma Ata pledges: Is devolution in Pakistan an opportunity for rekindling primary health care?", *Department of Community Health Sciences, Aga Khan University, Karachi*, available at .http://www.jpma.org.pk/PdfDownload/1096.pdf (accessed June 16, 2010).

USAID (undated), "Health Systems 20/20 - Pay for performance", available at. http://www.healthsystems2020.org/section/topics/p4p.

USAID (undated), "Pay for Performance: Improving Maternal Health Services in Pakistan", available at http://www.healthsystems2020.org/content/resource/detail/2577/

USAID Pakistan (undated), "Voucher Programme Saving Lives in Dadu, Sindh", available at. http://www.healthsystemspak.com/documents/HANDSSSFinal.pdf

USAID primer for policymakers (2006), "Vouchers for Health: A Focus on Reproductive Health and Family Planning Services", 2006.Washington DC.

World Health Organisation (undated), "Regional Health Systems Observatory - Health Systems Reforms", available at http://gis.emro.who.int/HealthSystemObservatory/PDF/Pakistan/Health%20system%20reform.pdf

World Health Organization (undated), "Demand Side Financing Maternal Health Voucher Scheme in Bangladesh", available at http://www.searo.who.int/LinkFiles/FCH_d3-4voucher-scheme-Ban.pdf

8

Universal Health Care and Private Provision in the Philippines

Bienvenido "Nonoy" Oplas, Jr.[1]

I. Introduction

The pursuit of providing universal healthcare (UHC) (or "Kalusugan Pangkalahatan" in Filipino) to each of the nearly 100 million Filipinos is a noble goal. It is a goal that is shared by all stakeholders in the country.

The big question is how to attain it at the most efficient and least costly way, both to the government and households and taxpayers. The dominant thinking is to follow the European and North American models of universal healthcare, in which government takes the dominant role in the healthcare system, and most costs are underwritten by the public purse. This explains the rising budget for the Department of Health at the national level, and health spending at the Local Government Unit levels. This is not currently sustainable as the Philippine government is still heavily indebted, even though the debt/GDP ratio has improved compared to a decade ago.

Table 1: Government Gross Debt as Percent of GDP, Selected Asian Economies

(2012 data are projections)

Country	*2005*	*2010*	*2012*	*Country*	*2005*	*2010*	*2012*
Singapore	93.5	101.2	106.2	Japan	186.4	215.3	236.6
Laos	85.7	61.8	54.1	Taiwan	34.9	38.1	41.7
Malaysia	42.7	51.0	53.0	Korea	28.7	33.4	33.5
Vietnam	41.2	54.0	50.4	Hong Kong	33.8	34.6	33.1
Thailand	47.4	42.6	44.2	China	17.6	33.5	22.2
Myanmar	82.5	53.0	43.5				
Philippines	59.2	43.5	41.5	India	81.8	68.0	67.6
Cambodia	36.0	29.1	28.5	Pakistan	63.5	61.6	62.4
Indonesia	46.3	26.9	23.9	Nepal	51.9	35.4	28.3

Source: IMF, World Economic Outlook, Database October 2012, www.imf.org

The Philippine government recognises this fiscal constraint and has limited its additional health subsidy to the "really poor".

II. Demand for Healthcare in the Philippines

The Philippines is the 12th biggest country in the world in terms of population size. From only 60.7 million in 1990, it has grown to 92.1 million in the August 2010 survey, and it is projected to reach 100 million in 2015 or 2016. The population is growing at around 1.7 million people a year. At this rate, it is like creating an equivalent of a new Singapore (5 million) approximately every three years, or a new Hong Kong (7 million) approximately every 4 years.

It is a generally young country with about 43 percent of the population just 19 years old or below. So dealing with pediatric diseases is an important consideration for the country. Senior citizens (60+) number nearly seven million, or about seven percent of the total population. The advantage is that the working age population, those who are between 20 to 59 years old, comprise about half of the total. Life expectancy is not high compared to many other countries but there is improvement compared to several decades ago.

Table 2: Philippine Demographics, 2000 to 2013

Indicators	*2000*	*2010*	*Proj. 2013*
Population, Million	76.50	92.10	97.45
Growth rate, Percent	2.34	1.90	(assumpt.1.9)
19 yrs old and below, Million	36.33	40.39	42.74
Share to total, Percent	47.5	43.9	
20-59 yrs old, Million	35.61	45.48	49.48
Share to total, Percent	46.5	49.4	
60 and above, Million	4.56	6.23	6.23
Share to total, Percent	6.0	6.8	
Life expectancy, years M/F		67/73	

Sources:
(a) 2000, 2010, National Statistics Office (NSO, www.census.gov.ph);
(b) 2013 numbers are author's projections assuming the same 1.9 percent growth rate;
(c) Life expectancy from WHO.

The government is aligning its poverty reduction, healthcare and other targets with those of the United Nations' Millennium Development Goals (MDGs). It is expected that targets relating to infant and child mortality will be met within four years. Maternal mortality remains a major problem, and still occurs at a rate more than four times the target.

In addition, the prevalence rate for tuberculosis remains high although TB detection and cure rates have improved and are close to the MDG targets.

Table 3: Basic Healthcare Targets

Indicators	***2011***	***Target 2016***
Infant Mortality Rate (IMR, (per 1,000 live births)	22	19
Under 5 Mortality Rate (U5MR, (per 1,000 live births)	30	26.7
Maternal Mortality Rate (MMR, (per 100,000 live births)	221	52
TB Prevalence Rate (per 100,000)	502 (2010)	387
TB Case Detection Rate (percent)	73	90
TB Cure Rate (percent)	84	90
Malaria Morbidity Rate (per 100,000)	9.5	4
Malaria Mortality Rate (per 100,000)	0.01	< 0.03
HIV AIDS Prevalence Rate (percent of population)	< 1	< 1

Source: Department of Health (DOH), presentation at the Senate for its 2013 proposed budget.

The Maternal Mortality Ratio was already declining until about 2006 at only 162 but suddenly went up as of 2011 to 221. In many rural areas or even in urban but economically depressed areas, many mothers still insist on giving birth inside their homes where possible infections are high and post natal care is poor. This situation is among the major reasons cited by the various camps that support government sponsored population control, aka "Reproductive Health" (RH) bill, that there should be more maternal health clinics, more condoms, pills and injectable contraceptives provided by the government.

Figure 1: Maternal Mortality Rate per 100,000 live births

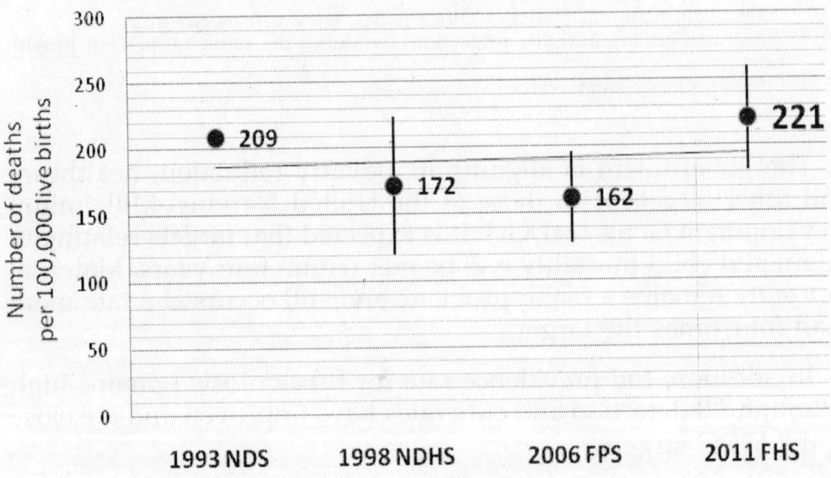

Source: Family Health Survey (FHS) 2011 (NSO, DOH, USAID)

III. Government Supply of Healthcare

The government is the main supplier of healthcare services nationwide. Here is a short outline of government involvement and provision of this service.

1. National Government:

The Department of Health (DOH) and its attached bureaus and agencies, attached hospitals and rural drugstores, which are collectively known as "Botikang Barangay" (BnB), is the single biggest agency to provide various healthcare services to Filipinos.

DOH hospitals are affiliated with the Philippine Hospital Association (PHA, www.pha. ph), although many members there are private hospitals.

The Philippine Health Insurance Corporation (PHIC or PhilHealth), created by Republic Act (RA) 7875 or the National Health Insurance Act of 1995, as amended by RA 9241 in 2004, is the main agency tasked to implement UHC.

Many other government agencies that are not directly health related have their own hospitals too. These include:

- University of the Philippines (UP), Philippine General Hospital (UP-PGH), UP Health Services
- Department of National Defense (DND):(a) Armed Forces of the Philippines (AFP)Medical Center, (b) Philippine Air Force General Hospital, (c) Camp Gen. Emilio Aguinaldo Station Hospital, (d) Veterans Memorial Medical Center, (e) Presidential Security Group Station Hospital, (f) Manila Naval Hospital, (g) Fprt del Pilar Station Hospital, Baguio City.
- Department of Interior and Local Government (DILG) Philippine National Police (PNP) General Hospital
- Department of Justice (DOJ) Bureau of Corrections' (BUCOR)'s New Bilibid Prisons Hospital

Some government corporations like the Philippine Charity Sweepstakes Office (PCSO) and the Philippine Amusement and Gaming Corporation (PAGCOR) also provide limited hospitalisation cover for the poor, but they must queue long hours or even days, to get PCSO guarantee. This office also provides free ambulance services to certain LGUs.

Other Departments and government corporations also provide occasional medical and dental missions to poor and rural households.

2. Local Government Units (LGUs)

Many LGUs have their own hospitals, especially in the cities and provinces (Ospitalng Maynila, Ospitalng Makati, Ospitalng Muntinlupa). Most of the 80 provinces in the country have their own provincial hospitals. In addition, there are also District hospitals that are maintained by the DOH or the LGU where they are located.

Then there are Barangay or village health centers and Rural Health Units (RHUs) under the city or municipal governments.

III. Private Supply of Healthcare

There are several hundred private hospitals nationwide. Many if not all of them are affiliated with the Private Hospitals Association of the Philippines, Inc. (PHAPI, www.phap-ph.org): 283 in Luzon including Metro Manila, 59 in Visayas, 171 in Mindanao. The more prestigious names are all in Metro Manila, for example the Makati Medical Center, St. Lukes Medical Center, Medical City and Asian Hospital.

Several Health Maintenance Organizations (HMOs) compete for subscribers and have their own health facilities, or have a referral system with private hospitals.

Big companies, schools and universities also have their own clinics and health facilities with their own set of physicians and other health professionals.

Then there are the industry associations and professional organizations. Pharmaceutical and Healthcare Association of the Philippines (PHAP) is the federation of mostly multinationals and drug innovator companies. Many members of this federation were adversely affected by the drug price control policy of 2009 where their most popular drugs were mandatorily discounted by 50 percent. The big drugstore chain Mercury Drugstore is also a member of PHAP.

The Philippine Chamber of Pharmaceutical Industry (PCPI) is the umbrella organization of national and generic drug manufacturers in the Philippines, led by United Laboratories (UL), the biggest pharmaceutical company in the country with 24 percent share of total market value.

Mercury is the biggest drugstore chain in the country cornering around 60 percent of the total retail market. The other chain drugstores are Watsons, The Generics Pharmacy, Rose Pharmacy, South Star / Mansons, and Generika. The small, independent and non-chain outlets are affiliated with the Drug Store Association of the Philippines (DSAP).

Among the health professionals, the leading organizations are the Philippine Medical Association (PMA) for the physicians and specialists, the Philippine Pharmacists Association (PPhA) and the Philippine Nurses Association (PNA).

There is also a big role played by civil society. There are dozens of health NGOs and charities that directly provide health services. Among them are Botika Binhi, Alternative Health, Philippine Pharmaceutical Foundation (PPF) and so on.

There is also close to 800 Rotary clubs nationwide under 10 Districts of the Rotary International. Many clubs have regular health and medical missions every year, some of which are focused on certain diseases like cleft palette, child immunization, or children with Childhood Congenital Diseases (CGD). The "Gift of Life" program is a special project of Rotary for this case.

In one joint meeting of several Rotary Clubs in District 3830 in 2012 attended by the author, several rich Rotarians contributed some PhP 1.2 million (nearly US$ 29,000) in just one sitting for the "Gift of Life" project. The beneficiaries are poor children in the government-owned Children's Hospital.

Other civic organizations that conduct non-profit medical missions and programmesinclude the Lions Club, Masons, Jaycees, Kiwanis, etc., church-based organizations like Couples for Christ (CfC), and non-health professional organizations.

IV. Government Failure in Attaining UHC

Government has long been involved in healthcare delivery and organization in the Philippines, since perhaps the Spanish and American colonial periods. For this paper, we will start from 1969 where a big, early attempt at UHC for all was made with the Medicare Act.

Box 1: The Health Framework in Philippines

1969	Medicare Act.
1979	Adoption of Primary Health Care System to deliver UHC for all, in line with the Alma Ata Convention of 1998.
1983	EO 851 -Integration of Public Health and Hospital Services.
1988	RA 667- Philippine Generics Act.
1991	RA 7160 - Local Government Code, devolution of primary healthcare function to local government units.
1992	RA 7432 - Granting benefits and special privileges to senior citizens.
1995	RA 7875 - National Health Insurance Act, which also created the Philippine Health Insurance Corporation (PhilHealth). (The creation of PhilHealth in 1995 was a clear and explicit admission that the earlier experiment on UHC through MediCare was a failure. Huge inefficiencies and corruption brought down that agency.)
1999	Health Sector Reform Agenda (HSRA).
2008	RA 7502, Cheaper Medicines Law, amended the intellectual property code (IPC), institutionalized compulsory licensing (CL) and drug price regulation and control.
2009	Maximum retail price (MRP) imposed, mandatory 50 percent price cut for selected branded medicines through an Executive Order.
2010	RA 9994, Expanded Senior Citizens Act of 2010, amending RA 7432.

Despite all of these attempts, out-of-pocket (OOP) spending for healthcare remained high, at almost half of the estimated total health expenditure in the country as of 2005 (Figure 2).

Figure 2: Distribution of Total Health Expenditures (THE), 2005

Philippine National Health Accounts, out of estimated P180 B (3.3 percent of GDP):

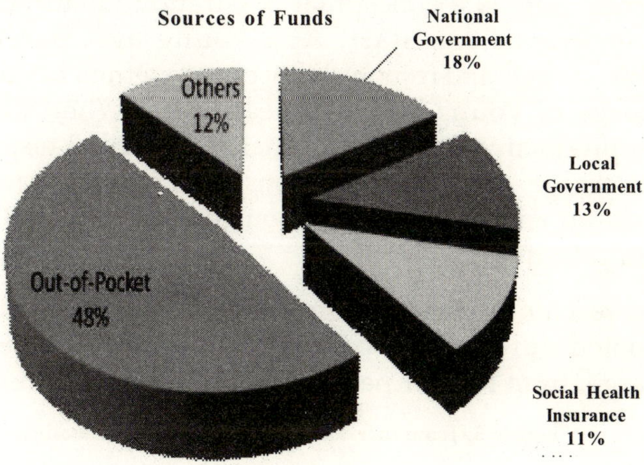

Source: Lagrada, 2010.

The share of social health insurance via PhilHealth rose marginally from 5 percent in 1997 to 11 percent in 2005, still a small portion ten years after its creation.

A paper presented by Dr. Suzette Lazo during to the MeTA Philippines national summit on UHC in September 2010, made this assessment and admission of government failure in the health sector:

> *Thirty years of Health Sector Reforms, starting with the adaptation of devolution of health care delivery has not found the Philippines in the list of Healthy Nations. Even with the inception of the Health Sector Reform Agenda in 1999, progress to the goal of Universal Health Care is painstakingly slow, if at all occurring... With the initiatives set on paper and in programs, we have not gone far as a nation in attaining the goals of 'Health for all Filipinos'. Until now, the ideal of Universal Health Care is but a dream for the nation.*

Dr. Lazo was Director of the Food and Drugs Administration (FDA) from mid 2010 to mid-2012.

V. Illustrations of various Healthcare financing

Before discussing the existing healthcare financing in the Philippines, here is a conceptual illustration identifying where health insurance can start. At a young age, parental and guardians' savings and responsibility plus government subsidy will take charge of young people's healthcare. When the person becomes productive enough, personal and parental responsibility will take charge; government responsibility in healthcare can just be an add-on and not a primary source of healthcare financing, except in catastrophic diseases.

Upon reaching retirement and/or old age, savings that were accumulated during a person's higher productivity period will take charge, from regular pension to old age health insurance.

Figure 3: Insurance Payment and Subsidy timeline

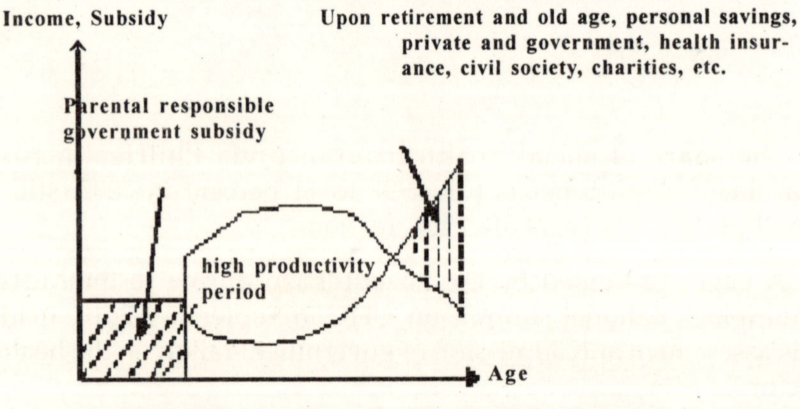

So people with high lifestyle-related diseases should save up more. The cost of treatment at the "tail" or right side can be equal to or larger than savings from the middle or higher productivity period, especially for cases of catastrophic diseases or complicated cancer cases. Family or clan savings and support from civil society charities will be needed to augment resources pooled from personal savings, and private and government health insurance.

Healthcare, like food, education, housing, information, etc. has costs. It cannot simply be provided "for free" out of thin air. Somebody has to pay for it at various stages of one's life.

We now explore the existing and proposed reforms in the Philippine healthcare financing system.

First, healthcare is divided into outpatient and inpatient services. For patients brought to private hospital emergency rooms (ERs), financing for outpatient services is usually administered via HMOs, LGUs, and Out-of-Pocket (OOP) for those who have no private health insurance or LGU health card.

Inpatient services are the main job of PhilHealth but coverage is limited (only P500 is available per day for a hospital bed), and the balance is shouldered by those mentioned above as financing the outpatient services. Other government agencies like DSWD, PCSO, also give limited cash cover for the balance.

Figure 4: Current Situation, Health Spending

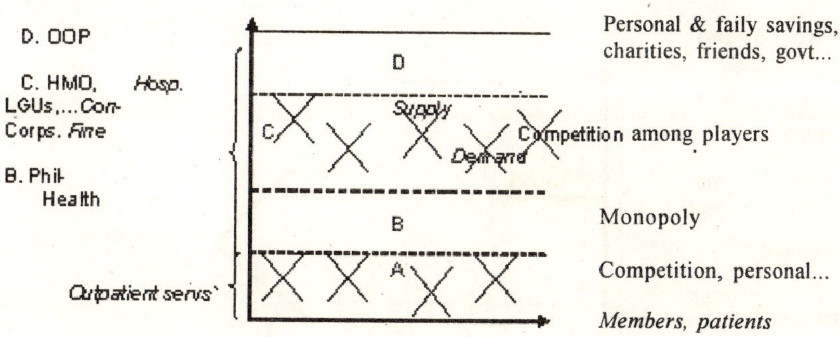

The portion that is socialized, nationalized and monopolized - by the Philippine Health Insurance Corporation (PhilHealth) - is relatively small. The bulk of healthcare spending comes from the private sector and OOP spending by the person, family and friends. Private charities such as foundations, civic and church organizations, hospital charities, etc. can further subsidize OOP spending.

Let's look at the proportion each of these sources of healthcare funding would contribute where a patient's total hospitalisation bill is US $10,000: PhilHealth provides about $2,000, HMO provides about $5,000 (depending on the insurance package), and the patient's family, friends and charities will provide the remaining $3,000.

Government welfare and charity programs as implemented by the DOH, Department of Social Welfare and Development (DSWD), Philippine Charity Sweepstakes Office (PCSO), and LGUs also augment financing for the poor. Some rich LGUs have their own provincial or city hospitals, where they give free or highly-subsidized healthcare for residents of their province or city.

The present condition is highly disadvantageous to the poor because of the huge OOP expenses. So recently, the DOH budget was increased to pay for the annual contribution of poor households to PhilHealth.

Figure 5: Dominant Proposal, Larger PhilHealth Role

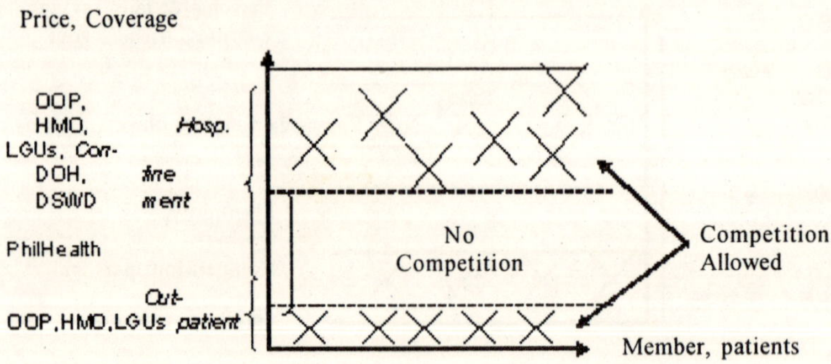

The prevailing and dominant proposal to better achieve UHC is to reform PhilHealth to make it even bigger and wealthier, towards a more centralised agency with much wider coverage and services.

The existing premium or mandatory contributions and coverage will be increased to cover outpatient and related services, and larger subsidies for hospital confinement cases, in order to reduce OOP expenses for the poor.

Competition among private providers of healthcare like the corporate and non-profit health maintenance organizations (HMOs) will be reduced as a number of their existing services to their clients and patients will be taken over by an enlarged, more powerful and wealthier PhilHealth. Health insurance competition among LGUs will also be reduced as the national government takes on a bigger role and involvement.

Increased coverage means increased monthly mandatory contributions by people who were made mandatory members by the law. And proposals are being put forward which would mean that those not previously covered by the mandatory contributions - such as the overseas Filipino workers (OFWs) - will soon be covered, meaning they cannot leave the country unless they sign up to the mandatory contributions.

A second, more radical position is to call for the national government, in co-ordination with LGUs, to finance and manage free or highly subsidised healthcare services to the public, from outpatient to inpatient services. This rights-based approach can be seen in Cuba, the United Kingdom and Canada.

For the advocates of this model, the profit motive under capitalism is incapable of providing healthcare for the poor. Thus, government should take over most if not all aspects of healthcare - drugs manufacturing and/or trading, hospitals and clinics, drugstores and drug retailing, hiring of health professionals, and so on.

This proposal is most likely inappropriate for a country such as the Philippines, which is characterized by a weak rule of law and highly politicized culture. As can be seen from the other major public endeavours that have been undertaken by the government, such as the new Manila airport, there is no assurance that more government involvement in healthcare would automatically translate into Universal Health Care.

A third way is to limit the government's role in healthcare to those areas where it has comparative advantage, such as: standard setting, regulation, dealing with infectious or communicable diseases, pediatric diseases, and children and adults with physical or mental limitations. The rest of the population should be given free choice and option where to get their health insurance.

The ultimate goal is the attainment of UHC for more Filipinos, not more government involvement per se.

Figure 6: More Private Provision and Competition, PhilHealth Status Quo

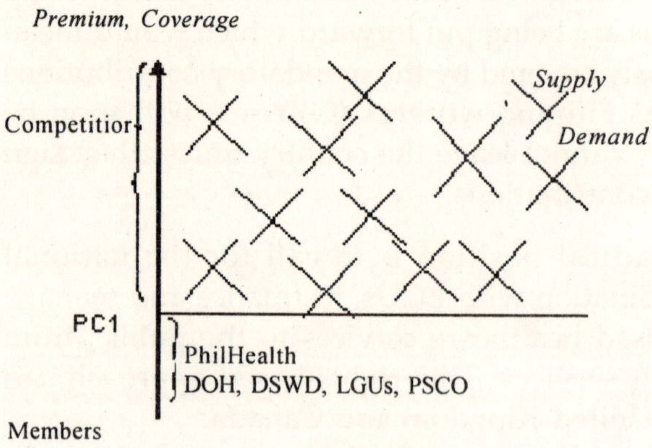

This would mean more competition above the services that PhilHealth will not cover – like outpatient services, diagnostic tests, annual general check-up, and dental services. PhilHealth would not be abolished nor be privatized; it would remain as a government owned and controlled corporation providing health insurance for members in cases of hospital confinement for at least 24 hours. There are administrative, practical and political benefits to PhilHealth remaining as is. The government could simply allow the emergence of more potential players, especially corporate and non-profit HMOs, and the expansion of existing ones.

This could be achieved by introducing a voucher system in healthcare and privatizing many of the public hospitals. The government could use the money saved from no longer having to sustain and subsidise public hospitals on issuing vouchers to all households.

The government would distribute two types of voucher to all households. Type A will be non-transferable, non-cashable and could only be used to purchase health insurance from the large number of private providers (hospitals, HMOs, etc.). This type can be valued at say, P 2,000 per person per year. Thus, a five-member household will receive P 10,000 per year. The family can choose a PhP 16,000 family health insurance premium, use the voucher and pay the P 6,000 extra, or solicit private donations to cover the gap.

Type B voucher will be transferable but non-cashable. Richer people could, if they so wish, donate this to their house helper/s or family driver/s to help them get a more comprehensive health insurance without forking out extra cash.

LGUs could also issue their own vouchers to their local residents as an addition to the national voucher. Or they could continue operating their city or provincial hospitals and pay for their costly maintenance. Or LGUs could contract with a big health insurance firm for a fixed amount and this firm will cover all residents for that city or province's specified minimum services.

The poor can further tap or approach private charities and health NGOs through the latter's medical missions, or by asking for additional insurance cover so that poor households with special or high demand for their sickly family member/s can get an insurance with larger healthcare coverage.

Competition among many private healthcare providers is the least costly, least bureaucratic, and most flexible way of regulating those providers and protecting the public without imposing high fiscal burden on taxpayers, and introducing further layers of politicisation in healthcare.

The food sector is a good example of the model proposed here. There are no government owned restaurants or "carinderia", no government-owned supermarkets, bakeries or butcher's shops. Instead, there are hundreds of food chains and food distributors around the country, each with their own unique or trusted brands.

There is market segmentation. Various health insurance providers, like health maintenance organizations (HMOs), be they corporate or cooperative, or local government, will offer different health insurance coverage for different people depending on their budget. The important point is that everyone should have health insurance.

Those who have a healthy lifestyle may purchase what the health voucher will cover, say P 2,000 a year per person, to cover the annual general check-up plus a pre-agreed number of medical appointments per year. Those who have an unhealthy lifestyle should get more expensive medical insurance. This way, the burden of those who are less responsible about their body will not be borne by the general taxpayers, but by the patients themselves, their family and their health insurance providers. This would have an additional benefit of reducing tobacco and alcohol use, and unhealthy eating, without extensive government intervention into those markets.

The various healthcare systems would not be provided exclusively by corporate entities. A "smorgasbord" of various private players - corporate (for profit) and non-profit charities (local and foreign) - would provide various healthcare services to the people. There would be no national or central healthcare agency, meaning the existing government healthcare agencies would be abolished - and with them large amounts of administrative savings.

To summarize the above options and scenario, here is how they would appear in a spectrum from the left to center to the right. The five letters correspond to the five graphs presented above.

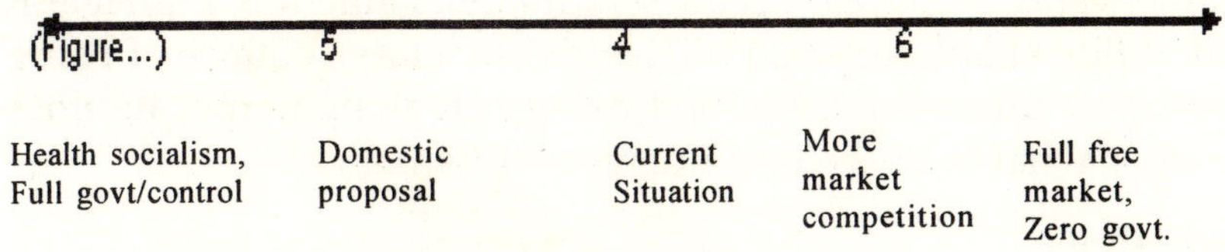

Porter and Telsberg (2010) made this interesting observation about the role of competition in healthcare:

> *In healthy competition, relentless improvements in processes and methods drive down costs. Product and service quality rise steadily. Innovation leads to new and better approaches, which diffuse widely and rapidly. Uncompetitive providers are restructured or go out of business. Value-adjusted prices fall, and the market expands. This is the trajectory common to all well-functioning industries - computers, mobile communications, banking, and many others.*
>
> *In any industry, competition should drive up value for customers over time as quality improves and costs fall. It is often argued that healthcare is different because it is complex; because consumers have limited information; and because services are highly customised. Health care undoubtedly has these characteristics, but so do other industries where competition works well. For example, the business of providing customized software and technical services to corporations is highly complex, yet, when adjusted for quality, the cost of enterprise computing has fallen dramatically over the last decade.*

It is the cost-minimization behaviour by competing players that will benefit patients and the public over the long-term. Healthcare providers who manage to significantly bring down their operational costs will be able to offer better healthcare for the public at a lower price, undercutting other competitors. Ultimately, the public and patients benefit as they will have more options to choose among many healthcare providers.

The same cannot be said if there is one huge provider like the government-owned PhilHealth. Giant bureaucracies are usually slow in adapting to changing behaviour and preferences by the customers and the public. As the senior management of PhilHealth are all political appointees, PhilHealth has a large chance of being captured by interest groups, and being run along corporate lines instead of what is in the best interests of its patients.

Conclusions

Universal Health Care (UHC), the idea that everyone should have some form of health insurance coverage, is a noble, plausible and attainable goal. There is no debate about it as even advocates of a free market can sympathise with that goal. The debate is limited to the most appropriate role for government and its agencies to achieve that goal.

Current discourse in the Philippines is heavily weighted towards an increased role for government in the provision of Universal Health Care, even though many decades of travel in this direction have failed to achieve this goal. Recent progress towards the health-related Millennium Development Goals is likely to be more a function of increased economic growth and higher incomes among the poor, rather than the outcomes of government intervention.

This chapter has argued that a more market-oriented provision of health services will best attain the UHC goal. The shift from direct provision to indirect provision via healthcare vouchers given to people will help in this direction. Market segmentation of healthcare financing via further health insurance deregulation will also help.

Inequalities in health can often be as much a result of lifestyle as an inability or otherwise to pay for healthcare. A person who may be rich but abuses his body will almost certainly suffer from disease earlier than someone who is poor but has led a more abstemious life. No amount of higher government subsidies can solve the problem of bad personal health if such outcomes are self-inflicted, and health reform in the Philippines should reflect this principle.

Note

1. President, Minimal Government Thinkers Inc., Philippines.

References

Department of Health (2012), "Proposed 2013 Budget", presented at the Senate, Philippines.

International Monetary Fund (2012), "World Economic Outlook", October 2012 Database, www.imf.org

Lagrada, Liezel, MD (2010), *Principles of Social Solidarity, Equity, Quality Assurance and Cost-Containment*, presentation at UP Asian Center, 14 April.

Lazo, Suzette (2010), "A People-Centered Health Sector Reform Agenda", Unpublished paper distributed during the "National Summit on Transparency and Governance in Universal Healthcare", September 16-17, 2010, Asian Institute of Management (AIM), Makati City. Jointly sponsored by MeTA Philippines and AIM.

National Statistics Office, Government of Philippines, www.census.gov.ph

Oplas, Bienvenido Jr. (2011), "Health Choices and Responsibilities", Quezon City: Central Book Supply, Inc.

Porter, Michael E. Porter and Elizabeth Olmsted Teisberg (2010), "Redefining Competition in Healthcare", available on http://www.asiahealthspace.com/2010/07/21/redefining-competition-in-healthcare/ (accessed on November 12, 2012).

9

ON THE DEVELOPMENT OF THE PRIVATE HOSPITALS IN CHINA

Feng Xingyuan, Jing Chaoliang, Yu Hui and Philip Stevens[1]

I. Introduction

It has been nearly 30 years since private hospitals reemerged in the People's Republic of China, and they currently play an increasingly important role in the provision of healthcare to Chinese citizens.[2] By the end of 2011 there were 457,000 private medical institutions across China, constituting 47.9% of the total medical institutions, but comprising only 9.7% of total hospital beds of the country. More specifically, there are 9,097 private hospitals, whose medical service covers mere 9.1% of total care in China.[3] The government envisages a far greater role for private hospitals, with its "12th Five-Year Plan" expressing an ambition to increase the share of private hospital beds to 20% nationwide.[4]

The figures above lead to two assumptions. On the one hand, private hospitals in China are in great market demand; but on the other, they face enormous barriers to being able to supply that demand. This essay sets out the evidence behind these assumptions and examines why private hospitals have been able to capitalize on demand, and what barriers they must overcome if they are to increase to the quantity desired by the government.

II. Chinese public hospitals' variety of failures leave opportunities for the private hospitals

Just as with the market provision of any other service, the emergence and recent growth of the Chinese private hospital sector is a result of the failure of public hospitals to supply the demand for medical services. At the moment, the two most common terms used in popular discourse about healthcare are "difficult to have access to" and "unaffordable for qualified medical services" (or "*kanbingnan*" and "*kanbinggui*" in the Chinese language). Of course, this description is not strictly correct since many high ranked Communist Party officials are able to enjoy free, high quality medical services. Research carried out by the Chinese Academy of Science showed that these officials (reported to number around 8.5 million) consume 80% of all publically-provided medical resources every year,[5] leaving few resources left over to provide care to the remaining 1.2 billion Chinese citizens. To a large extent, public hospitals have been captured by the bureaucratic and political elite. Politically unconnected patients, who in fact comprise the majority of Chinese usually have to pay dearly to access public healthcare that is supposed to be free – hence, the phrase "kanbinggui"(near-to-unaffordable qualified medical service).

This situation is compounded by the reluctance by public hospital managers to expand, even when they have sufficient inputs from the government. According to Ren Lingyun, the reasons behind this lie in a desire by managers to create an illusion of scarcity, in order to retain their privileged position in society. Simultaneously, it is socially advantageous for managers to maintain the impression they act in the public interest.[6] This artificial constraint has the doubly negative effect of making it harder for new medical graduates to find positions in public hospitals, while making it extremely difficult for ordinary citizens to obtain care from the public sector. For example, it is common to find patients or their families sitting up the whole night in the lobby of a public hospital, queuing for a registered admission ticket to be seen by a specialist. In some cities, say, in Beijing, there is a black market for registered admission tickets in which they can be bought and re-sold like a commodity. One of the authors' friends once spent 500 yuan on a registered admission ticket for Jishuitan Hospital of Beijing from some ticket touts even though the nominal ticket price was less than 10 yuan. No wonder, the other common phrase people use to describe Chinese public medical services is *kanbingnan*!

Ironically, the lack of supply of healthcare for ordinary citizens via the public sector has created an enormous market opportunity for the private sector. This opportunity has been heightened by the continued economic growth of recent decades, with people now looking beyond their immediate day-to-day survival to a desire for better social services such as health and education. In addition, the baby-boom following the Second World War has now formed a huge population of senior citizens, all demanding increasing amounts of healthcare, while environmental pollution has also created increased demand for healthcare which the public sector is unable to supply. All of these conditions present opportunities for Chinese private hospitals to emerge and develop.

III. Private hospitals have unique comparative advantages

Unlike some developed countries where some private hospitals might be sponsored by a wealthy philanthropist or charitable organization, Chinese private hospitals are almost exclusively concerned with profit making, no different from private enterprises in other industries.[7] This clarity of purpose should, in principle, give rise to efficiencies in management, as it is in managers' self-interest to reduce operational costs wherever possible, without compromising quality of care. Public sector managers face no such pressures, by contrast. The problem of low-efficiency frequently seen in public hospitals is hardly seen in private ones.

There is also an incentive for doctors working in private hospitals to exhibit a more personalized approach to patients in order to retain and attract patients, rather than simply working to centrally-produced clinical guidelines as is the case with public sector doctors. So the doctors in private hospitals tend to be more patient-oriented.

Private hospitals in China tend to specialize in certain diseases rather than functioning as some comprehensive hospitals that many public hospitals are. So private hospitals can exploit their specialism to offer services more efficiently and cheaply, and adopt innovative technologies and clinical practices, while more monolithic public hospitals are often slow to adapt to changing patient demands and clinical research.

Despite the many theoretical advantages of private hospitals, it is true that there are certain challenges that need to be overcome, such as how to ensure equitable access, and how to prevent private providers from exploiting their advantages in information asymmetries with patients. These have been widely discussed elsewhere, and this essay will not dwell on them. Rather, it would be more interesting to examine which factors have prevented the private hospital sector in China from expanding more widely and are holding it back from achieving the government's target of it providing 20% of all care.

IV. Chinese private hospitals are facing external threats and internal weaknesses

Many scholars and practitioners in China have come to a consensus that private hospitals and public hospitals are opposing forces in the healthcare sector. Private hospitals have to date been put at a disadvantage by the government, as a result of the regulatory prioritization of public hospitals by government:

- Public hospitals are able to use land, premises, infrastructure and facilities free of charge, while the private ones are obliged to pay for any of them.
- Public hospitals are invariably free from paying any tax while the private ones are obliged to pay sales taxes, which can occupy over half of their marginal profits.[8]

- Public hospitals are more attractive to medical college graduates as well as to those highly skilled in medical service, while the private ones have to turn either to retired professionals or to those less trained.
- Public hospitals receive large sum of medical research funding from government, while private hospitals are not eligible for such funding.
- While nominally highly regulated, in reality public hospitals rarely have difficulty in passing officials checks or inspections, while private hospitals face enormous pressures from a wide range of bureaus.
- Public hospitals have access to special subsidies from government fiscal budget while the private ones have to earn their own living, which not only limits their ability to expand, but also leaves them exposed to liabilities from medical malpractice cases.
- Public hospitals will retain their market share regardless of the opinions of patients, while private hospitals often find it hard to enlarge their market shares, as alluded to at the beginning of this essay, and further illustrated in table 1.

Table 1: Dominance of Public Hospitals (Share in %, 2004-2010)

Year	*Number of Institutions* (%)	*Number of Beds* (%)	*Number of Medical Services Personal* (%)	*Turnover* (%)
2004	53.4	76.3	79.4	98.5
2005	52.8	76.2	79.4	97.7
2006	50.7	76.0	78.8	96.3
2007	49.5	76.7	79.0	86.5
2008	49.6	77.5	79.6	86.7
2009	47.6	77.4	79.0	86.4
2010	41.5	74.4	79.5	87.6

Data source: "China Health Statistics Annuals", 2005-2011.

While there is no doubt many other market advantages are held by the public sector, the overall point that private hospitals are severely discriminated against by the government seems uncontroversial. In addition to these government-imposed constraints, the private hospital sector suffers from a number of internal weaknesses, in particular a problem of accountability. According to Du Min, a doctor who knows private hospitals well, a number of Chinese private hospitals have been involved in some scandals involving dishonest practice, especially in the early days of the private sector's re-emergence in China. At that time, the patients visiting private hospitals were often from poorer socio-economic backgrounds and most definitely not Communist Party officials. Doctors at this time were not averse to exploiting information asymmetries in order to derive unnecessary fees from their patients.[9] These scandals have had a long-lasting and negative impact on the reputation of private hospitals, which in turned has constrained their growth. This "vicious circle" is represented diagrammatically in Figure 1.

Figure 1: The internal vicious circle constraining the growth of private hospitals

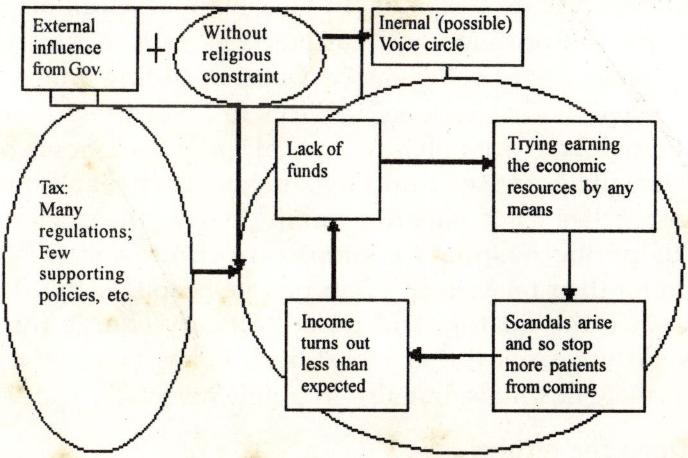

Du also puts forward some reasons for the scandals arising in some private hospitals, among which one key factor is worth quoting:

"In Christian countries, when people become very rich, they would consider doing some charity work and if such persons opened private hospital, chances will be few that they would sacrifice their conscience for making money. Even if some private hospitals are indeed profit-driven, they have to obey the rule of law ...However, in China, especially in People's Republic of China (i.e. since 1949), the government has kept dismantling the constraints by any religion in the name of atheism, which leads to a destructive result. That is, without the constraints of religious norms, people (including the private hospital owners) would feel that they seem able to commit anything they like, so that they would not feel any shame when they are engaged in anything corrupt, illegal or immoral. And moreover, since the rule of law is very weak in China, there are few constraints on unethical behaviour, which can explain why CCP cadres and the private hospital owners could sarcastically get on the same boat sometimes, forming certain interest groups."[10]

Such religiously unconstrained behaviours are common in some small private hospitals and clinics, especially in some unregistered clinics. However, it would be a misunderstanding that Du's remarks only relate to private hospitals. In fact, many doctors of public hospitals are performing unethical practices such as prescribing too many unnecessary or expensive drugs, or adding unnecessary and expensive 'body-checking' services to invoices so that they can get more rebate from pharmaceutical companies. Some public Chinese hospitals also sell drugs to patients directly, and it is also common practice for a patient's family to give the doctors and nurses of public hospitals a significant 'tip'to ensure better treatment for their relative. In larger private hospitals, this doesn't happen since the doctors and nurses already charge for their services. So we can see that moral decline has taken place not only in private hospitals, but also in public hospitals.

Suggestions for reform

As the previous sections suggest, there are a number of government-imposed and internal constraints to the successful and sustainable development of the private hospital sector in China.

With regards to the external constraints that arise from the uneven playing field imposed by the government, an obvious first step would be to create a more equal institutional environment in which both public and private hospitals are subject to the same rules, regulations and laws.

An important component of this would be to remove the unfair privileges of public hospitals, and create a clear division between the regulation and management of public hospitals in order to prevent the kinds of conflicts of interest currently seen. Public hospitals should also be removed from centralized administrative control, preferential treatment policies, including subsidies, in order to allow the market to play to its strengths in allocating resources including funding, recruitment and setting pay levels. Competition is necessary to inject innovation and efficiency into the current Chinese health system, which is currently characterized by an extraordinary inequality of access between the political and bureaucratic elite, and ordinary citizens. It will be impossible to achieve high quality universal healthcare in the current situation in which the public sector monopolizes resources largely for the benefit of Communist Party officials and their families. A vital step to end this monopoly would be to include private hospitals in the Social Medicare Insurance Scheme so that people could have more choices when seeking healthcare services besides the designated public hospitals.

Furthermore, it should not be seen as too radical to privatize the present state-owned hospitals, but a serious and feasible policy option if the Chinese government does want to create a competitive environment in which healthcare is directed towards the interests of the patient, rather than the provider. Privatization will involve significant readjustment, especially in the reorientation of government function, as a competitive health sector will not emerge unless there is a more level playing field between public and private.

The following table shows how the government has created systematic bias against the private sector since the founding of the People's Republic in 1949.

Table 2: The evolution of government's financial attitude toward public hospitals

Periods	*Financial policy on public hospitals*	*Notes*
1949-1955	Government bears all the cost of hospitals and all revenue are handed to the government.	Hospitals are nationalized.
1955-1960	As revenues are less than expenses, the government decides to provide subsidy up to certain limits.	Government is less interested in the ideological aspects of keeping hospitals nationalized, but keen to ensure that hospitals benefit certain interest groups.
1960-1979	Government continues to pay wages and salaries, but other operational expenses are met by hospitals themselves.	Hospitals are amongst the first losers from intensifying fiscal crises.
1979-2000	Hospitals are allowed to keep any positive balance from their revenues, while government subsidy is be generally dependent on numbers of beds and other factors.	As a result, many public hospitals become keen on making more profit since the profit would be at their own disposal, and the medical resources begin to be concentrated on larger hospitals.
2000- now	Government subsidy is oriented at certain categories of hospital expense, including but not limited to, officials' medical services, pensions, infrastructures, and scientific research, as well as the loss directly caused by government policies, etc.	Government appears to be indifferent as to whether hospitals are publically or privately owned, as long as they continue to provide services to officials and other elitea

Source: Huang Hua, an analysis into the financial input system of Chinese public hospitals, positive analysis, No.4, 2012.

From the evolution of government's attitude to public hospitals shown above, it can be seen that government policies concerning healthcare has been problematic ever since the state first became involved with healthcare some 60 years ago. The state has generally tried to exploit hospitals for its own advantages, while trying to avoid assuming the financial burdens of running public hospitals.

Although this paper is focused on private hospitals, this tendency of government to exploit public hospitals also, to an extent, explains why it has failed to create an institutional and regulatory environment that is conducive to the emergence of a robust and competitive private sector. Government has no incentive to create a dynamic private sector unless it can profit from that process, via taxation, even though such an agenda is in the interest of the patients who are currently ill-served by the public health system.

As for the internal weaknesses of Chinese private hospitals, the paper emphasizes two points. The way to overcome this is to move healthcare from an unresponsive state-dominated economy to at least a more patient-friendly 'mixed economy'. This requires two basic reforms: liberalizing the supply side to allow hospitals and providers to freely adapt to patient demand; and reforming the demand side to put purchasing power in the hands of the patients. The British government is moving towards limited supply side reform, but a more radical approach would involve:

- money following the patient, through 'credits' to spend at any private or public hospital of their choice;
- purchasers having a duty to their patient to buy from whichever provider offers the best service and value for money;
- removal of central controls and targets on hospitals and other healthcare suppliers, giving them complete freedom to manage their income, expenditure, staffing and procurement;
- privatization of under-performing government hospitals.

This would have the benefit of not requiring a 'revolution' away from the current system, as central government would gradually commission more and more from the private sector – this competition would in turn force state providers to improve their performance.

V. Conclusion

It is evident that the purely public hospitals cannot by themselves tackle growing demand for medical services from China's growing and more consumerist population, so greater involvement of the private sector is inevitable. Given government's contradictory attitude to the public hospitals, there are two barriers the government needs to remove if a high quality and equitable health care system is to be created. One barrier is the government's rigging of the playing field against private hospitals, which has created an unbalanced, anti-competitive situation. The other is government's desire to intervene in the operations of public hospitals, which dates back from the beginnings of the republic.

It is true that the State Council, the Chinese Administration, has issued a series of documents to promote the development of private hospitals and it is also true that the 12th five-year plan intends to foster greater competition in medical services. However, what really counts is not what the government says, writes or intends, but what the government actually does (or does not do). As analyzed above, the biggest constraints for Chinese private hospitals are located in two spheres. Internally, the private hospitals in China need to improve their professional discipline and ethics (as do the public hospitals); externally, they need to create an environment in which to compete with public hospitals that are run by the government but only benefit a select few.

Notes

1. Feng Xingyuan, Professor of Rural Development Institute of Chinese Academy of Social Sciences and Vice Director of Unirule Institute of Economics; Jing Chaoliang, a Ph. D. applicant in Renmin University of China; Yu Hui, Professor of Institute of Industrial Economics of Chinese Academy of Social Sciences; Philip Stevens, Executive Director, Emerging Markets Health Network.
2. The first private hospital in PRC (Yishou Hospital of Guangzhou) was founded in 1983.
3. http://www.fx120.net/chanjing/scfx/814975.html, accessed on 2012/10/2
4. http://news.xinhuanet.com/politics/2012-06/21/c_112270602.htm, accessed on 2012/10/2
5. http://news.163.com/06/0919/02/2RBLP7VO000120GU.html, accessed on 2012/10/2

6 http://www.chinareform.org.cn/society/Medical/Forward/201012/t20101215_54944_1.htm, accessed on 2012/10/4

7 There were many private hospitals which were sponsored by religious, philanthropist or charitable organizations before the founding of the People's Republic in 1949, which worked well. They were renationalized in the 1950s. They are ancestors of many large public hospitals.

8 http://finance.eastmoney.com/news/1355, 201207 13221814613.html, accessed on 2012/10/2.

9 http://www.haodf.com/zhuanjiaguandian/dolantin_65361495.htm accessed on 2012/10/2.

10 Ibid.

References

W. Wilson, *The Study of Public Administration*ÿJ. M. Shafritz, et al, *Classics of Public Administration*: The Dorsey Press, 1987.

John Locke, *Two Treatises of Government*, Cambridge University Press, 1960.

Thomas Hobbes, *Leviathan*, China Social Sciences Publishing House, 1999.

Plato, *The Republic*, trans. Alan Bloom. New York: Basic Books, p. 235.

Alexis de Tocqueville, *Democracy in America*, Liberty Fund Inc., 2010.

Huang Hua, *an analysis into the financial input system of Chinese public hospitals*, Positive Analysis, 2012, 4.

Meng Xiangsheng, *The Healthcare System Reform Abroad and the Lessons thereof on China, Journal of Tianjin Manager College*, 2012, 6.

Ren Lingyun, *the root causes of Kanbingnan and kanbinggui*, available on http://www.chinareform.org.cn/society/Medical/Forward/201012/t20101215_54944_1.htm (accessed on 2012/10/4).

Ministry of Health, PRC, *Further encouraging/directing the private capital to establish Private Medical Institutions*, available on http://news.xinhuanet.com/politics/2012-06/21/c_112270602.htm (accessed on 2012/10/2).

Anonymous reporter, Private Hospitals' market share, 9.1%, available on http://www.fx120.net/chanjing/scfx/814975.html (accessed on 2012/10/2).

Zhou Kai, *2 million CCP cadres on long-term leave,* available on http://news.163.com/06/0919/02/2RBLP7VO000120GU.html (accessed on 2012/10/2).

Zhong Kefen, *Private hospital: just a business for a few? available* on http://finance.eastmoney.com/news/1355,20120713221814613.html (accessed on 2012/10/2).

Du Min, *the ill conditions for developing private hospitals in China,* available on http://www.haodf.com/zhuanjiaguandian/dolantin_65361495.htm (accessed on 2012/10/2).

10

Helping the Private Sector To Help the Poor: Lessons from India

Debashis Chakraborty[1]

Introduction

India, one of the major developing countries in the world, has experienced an impressive growth trajectory since initiation of the Structural Adjustment Programme (SAP) in 1991, as recommended by the IMF. It has witnessed a GDP growth rate of around 7 percent consistently over the last decade, even during the recession years (GoI, 2012). The growth has been largely fuelled by the increasing outward orientation of the Indian economy. The country has enhanced its share in global merchandise exports from 0.62 per cent in 1999 to 1.67 per cent in 2011, while the same for service export increased from 1.00 per cent to 3.28 percent over the same period. Among India's service exports, IT-enabled and health services have emerged as major areas in recent years.

The healthcare industry in India has emerged as a major segment of the economy, with a growth rate of more than 13 per cent per annum over the last decade (Jain and Sinha, 2009). The domestic market is expanding rapidly, with economic growth in general and development of the tier-two and tier-three towns in particular. The major exports under this category includes: telemedicines, telediagnostics, medical transcription (Mode 1); medical tourism (Mode 2); and movement of Doctors, Nurses and Midwives etc. (Mode 4) It is estimated that India's share in the global medical tourism industry will reach around 3 per cent by the end of 2013 (HCI, 2011). Projections also reveal that the health industry will account for 6.1 percent of GDP by 2012 and provide employment to around 9 million people (Chanda, undated).

But how 'healthy' is the Indian healthcare system? To what extent does the government need to manage the development of this sector compared to allowing market forces to determine its development? This is indeed a debated topic in the Indian context, given the growing population size of India. Although the received wisdom demands a greater role for market forces in ensuring efficient healthcare service delivery, there exists considerable support for government intervention, especially for infrastructure creation.

However, no healthcare solution in India can be devised without active participation of the private sector. Raman (undated) notes that in India, 93 per cent of all facilities, 64 per cent of all beds, 80 per cent of doctors, 80 per cent of outpatients and 57 per cent of inpatients are in the private sector. Therefore, the government objective of expanding the healthcare delivery coverage can only be possible with active support from this segment.

While the growing volume of medical services export shows that the country is moving up the value chain and offering quality care, there is substantial scope for improving the domestic framework as well as infrastructure (Narayan, 2009). From a supply-side perspective, the Medical Council of India (MCI) currently recognises 205 medical colleges (and 65 more colleges have been permitted under section 10A of the Indian Medical Council Act (1956) which collectively produce approximately 28,000 qualified doctors annually. The MCI has recently granted approval to 21 new medical colleges, and the total number of MBBS seats in future is estimated to reach 39,785 (Indian Express, 2011). The graduating doctors, after completion of a compulsory internship, need to register with State Medical Councils or the Medical Council of India to practice medicine in the country. A similar network is there for the education of trained nurses as well. But are the numbers sufficient for fulfilling the country's requirement? Moreover, the coverage of health insurance in India has historically been poor, which prompted a recent World Bank study to recommend increasing health insurance coverage for both outpatient and inpatient care to aid households below the poverty line (Dhar, 2012).

In this context, the need for undertaking healthcare sector reforms including financing reforms in India has been long noted (Rao and Choudhury, 2012). The present study is arranged along the following lines: Firstly, a brief discussion on the healthcare infrastructure in India was undertaken through a cross-country comparison. Secondly, the shifting of government policy focus regarding healthcare delivery is noted and the implications of the recent Public-Private-Partnerships (PPP) in the national context are discussed. Finally, on the basis of the analysis, a few policy conclusions are drawn.

How 'developed' is India's Healthcare Infrastructure?

The preparedness of India to offer quality health services to the domestic population as well as to be engaged in trade in health services in the global market has been evaluated by comparing it with select developed and developing countries, with respect to a few healthcare related indicators. It is observed from Table 1 that public health expenditure expressed as a percentage of GDP in India is quite low, and has improved only marginally in the last decade. In comparison expenditure has improved considerably in Southeast Asian countries such as Malaysia and Thailand, or Brazil and Mexico in the Americas.

Table 1: Comparison of public expenditure on health, as % of GDP.

Country Name	*1995*	*2000*	*2005*	*2010*
India	*1.22*	*1.27*	*0.93*	*1.18*
Philippines	1.36	1.63	1.43	1.28
Indonesia	0.64	0.72	1.00	1.28
Malaysia	1.43	1.67	1.85	2.44
China	1.79	1.77	1.83	2.72
Thailand	1.66	1.91	2.29	2.91
Mexico	2.17	2.36	2.64	3.09
Brazil	2.86	2.89	3.28	4.24
World	5.48	5.34	5.70	6.52
Japan	5.71	6.25	6.56	7.83
European Union	6.76	6.58	7.01	8.06
United States	6.09	5.79	6.70	9.49

Source: World Development Indicators

As observed from Table 2, the low public expenditure coupled with the huge population size of the country, has produced quite low health expenditure per capita in global context, even with respect to the corresponding figure for several Asian neighbours. These statistics are indicative of the fiscal deficit experienced by the Government of India over the last two decades. The key question is, therefore, given the budget constraint; to what extent is the government willing to embrace private sector participation in the healthcare sector?

Table 2: Comparison of Health Expenditure Per capita (Current US $)

Country	*1995*	*2000*	*2005*	*2010*
India	*16.48*	*20.68*	*29.97*	*54.25*
Indonesia	20.86	15.84	26.84	76.89
Philippines	36.54	33.47	42.12	77.33
Thailand	98.66	66.84	94.90	179.15
China	21.31	43.72	80.58	220.88
Malaysia	125.68	128.12	222.07	367.92
Mexico	176.26	324.25	471.54	603.67
World	454.94	484.08	682.03	950.38
Brazil	316.36	265.19	387.27	990.39
European Union	1660.34	1497.42	2630.61	3368.31
Japan	2874.62	2827.45	2907.88	4065.42
United States	3747.69	4703.47	6258.60	8361.73

Source: World Development Indicators

Figures 1-3 looks into the improvement in health infrastructure in India regarding select developed and developing countries. Figure 1 reports the scenario for hospital bed per thousand persons during 1995-2002 and 2003-10. It is observed that while the figure has marginally improved for India in recent times, it is still not impressive on a global scale. The growth in health infrastructure in the country has failed to keep up with the pressure placed on it by the growth in population.

Figure 2 compares the number of health personnel employed in India with other countries. It is observed that the number of physicians per 1000 people has again improved for India in the recent period, but the achievement still looks modest in the global scale, especially with respect to other developing countries like Brazil, Mexico, Malaysia, the Philippines etc. A similar scenario is observed in the case of cross-country comparison on per capita availability of nurses and midwives from Figure 3 as well.

Finally, looking at the data for international comparison of out-of-pocket health expenditure (expressed as percentage of private expenditure on health) as reported in Figure 4, it is observed that the figures are also quite high in developing countries like India, China and Mexico. The observation implies that the reach of the health insurance network in India is still inadequate and there is considerable scope of further expansion.

Figure 1: Comparison of Hospital beds (per 1,000 people)

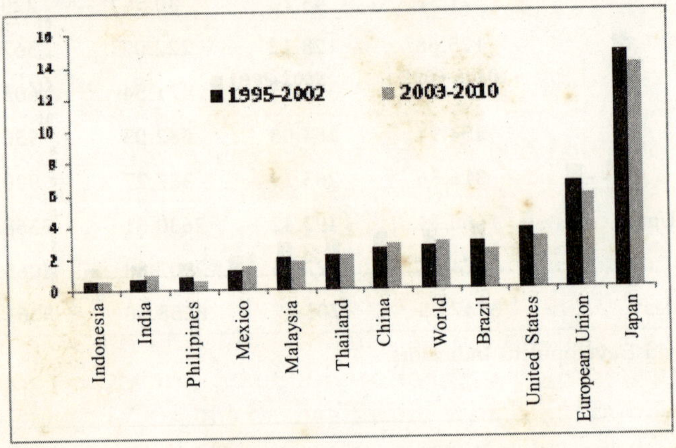

Source: Calculated from World Development Indicators data

Figure 2: Comparison of Physicians (per 1,000 people)

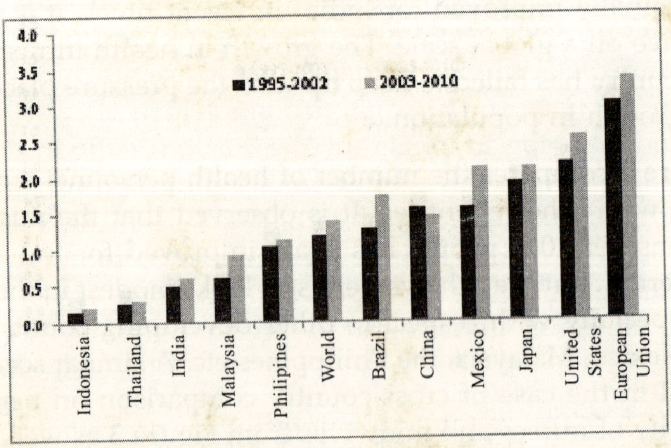

Source: Calculated from World Development Indicators data

Figure 3: Comparison of Nurses and Midwives (per 1,000 people)

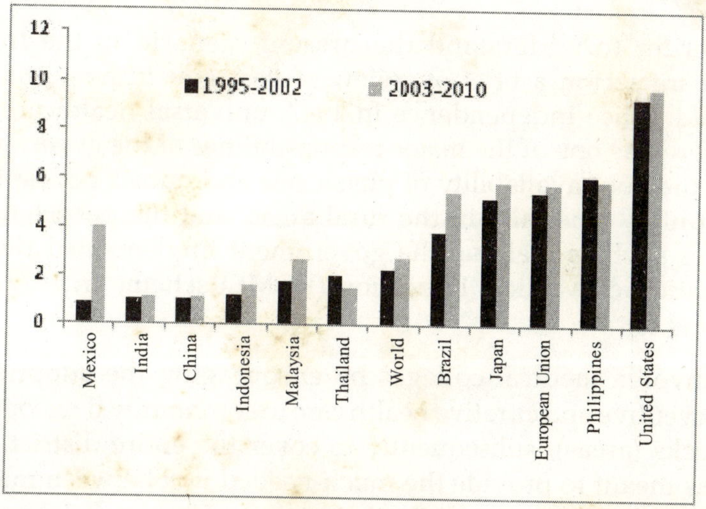

Source: Calculated from World Development Indicators data

Figure 4: Comparison of Out-of-pocket health expenditure (% of private expenditure on health)

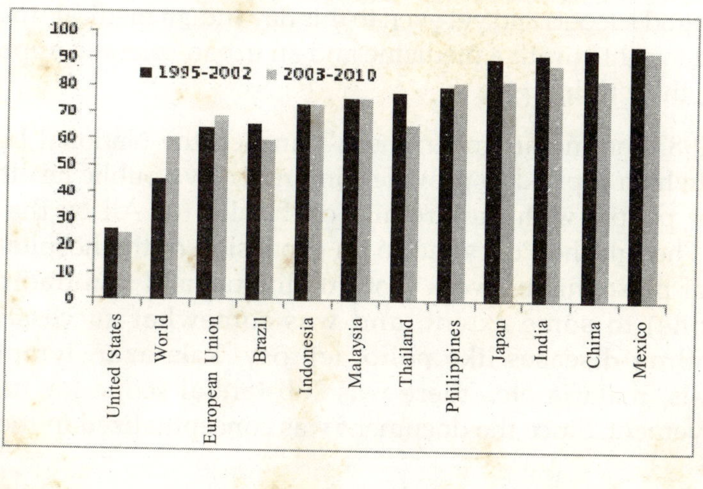

Source: Calculated from World Development Indicators data

The Government Policy Response: Pragmatic Prisoner of Ideology?

In order to understand the present scenario in the Indian healthcare sector, a brief overview of past government policy is required. Since independence in 1947, universal healthcare was considered as one of the major responsibilities of the government. Given the poor availability of physicians and nurses per capita in the country, especially in the rural areas, and the persistence of diseases such as malaria, the government implemented the Re-Orientation of Medical Education (ROME) scheme in 1977. The idea was to:

> '..involve medical colleges by encouraging the adoption of preventive and curative health care in community development blocks (areas), subsequently to cover the entire district. This was meant to provide the much-needed link between medical colleges and communities, being mutually beneficial to both by linking health care provision and referral for the community along with an opportunity for medical colleges to acquaint medical graduates to rural communities.' (Bangdiwala et al, 2011.)

In other words, reform through public and private sector health personnel was explored as a viable solution. However the initiative met limited success and yet even to this day Indian medical students are still taught curative medicine and an urban-oriented approach during their training.

In 1983 the Indian government launched the National Health Policy which aspired to provide comprehensive public healthcare to poor people with the promise of 'Health for All by the year 2000'. Though the Policy led to an expansion of the hospital and medical personnel network (both traditional and non-traditional medicine) to some extent, and was somewhat successful in controlling diseases like polio, leprosy, kala azar, lymphatic filariasis, malaria etc., there was substantial scope for further improvement. Since the document was conceptualized in the pre-liberalization period, pro-market reforms and medical service export were not included within its purview.

The fiscal mismanagement and the resulting budget constraint during the late 1980s forced the government to rethink its healthcare policy. Thomas and Krishnan (2010) note that during the Sixth Plan period (1980-85) a greater role for the private sector in securing a greater reach of healthcare to citizens was proposed for the first time. In line with the changed focus of the government, in 1986the hospital sector was recognized as an industry, thereby enabling the hospitals to raise capital from public ûnancial institutions. Moreover, customs duties on high-technology medical equipment were reduced, which consequently improved the quality of healthcare in Indian medical providers.

After the initiation of the structural adjustment programme in India from 1991 onwards, economic philosophy underwent another round of transformation. Tendulkar and Bhavani (2007) note that during the 8th Plan period the determination of the government to implement the reforms was strengthened. Pandav (2007) observes that health sector reform received a strong push in 1992 when the concept of free medical care was revoked, while the commitment for free or subsidized care for the Below Poverty Line (BPL) population was retained. Moreover, user charges were also introduced in the hospitals. However, while the government paved the way for private sector involvement to some extent, the resulting entry to mitigate the challenges was limited. In short, the expansion of private health network fell short of government expectations.

The stagnating healthcare framework forced the government to move towards yet another policy shift when the National Health Policy (2002) was introduced to bring Indian health network in line with the agendas of Millennium Development Goals (MDGs). In particular the document was quite pragmatic in terms of encouraging the outward orientation of the healthcare sector, as it strongly encouraged export of health services for payment to overseas patients, in order to capitalize on comparative cost advantages. It also promised that, "providers of such services to patients from overseas will be encouraged by extending to their earnings in foreign exchange, all fiscal incentives, including the status of 'deemed exports', which are available to other exporters of goods and services."Furthermore, in line with the liberalization drive, the participation of the civil society, namely that of the NGOs as well as domestic private sector, was strongly advocated by various sections of the document. Consequently, several options were highly recommended by the document, including privatization of existing public hospitals, creation of new private initiatives and subcontracting of public health centres to NGOs. (Chakraborty and Chakraborty, 2009.)

Baru (undated) has noted that the private initiatives led to the creation of both outpatient and inpatient facilities. Such entities promoted by single owners or partners (generally doctors) with between 5 to more than 100 beds emerged both in towns and cities as well as in peri-urban and rural areas. The reforms helped a number of private big hospitals like Wockhardt Group and Apollo to gain prominence, which catered to the needs of foreign patients as well (Chakraborty and Dilwaria, 2011). The ability to provide cost-effective healthcare solutions, availability of skilled healthcare professionals, and a reputation for treatment in advanced fields of healthcare enabled India to project itself as a 'low-cost, assured quality' health service exporter (Stokes, 2007). Foreign patients came mostly from South and West Asia and Africa, while non-resident Indians (NRIs) from various parts of the world also came back home for treatment. Foreign Direct Investment (FDI) inflow from abroad, as reported in Table 3, contributed significantly in fueling this outward orientation.

Table 3: Select Approved FDI in Hospitals by DIPP

Sl. No.	*Date*	*Indian company*	*Country of foreign investor*	*Foreign equity (Millions)* *Rs.*	*US $*
1	December 2002	Sir Edward Dunlop Hospitals, New Delhi	Canada	1,282.25	26.71
2	January 2004	Max Healthcare, New Delhi	Mauritius	316.21	6.63
3	January 2000	Dr. Ramayya's Pramila Hospitals Ltd, Hyderabad	UK-NRI	15.00	0.35
4	October 2001	Malabar Institute of Medical Sciences Hospital Ltd., Calicut	UAE	133.61	2.97
5	August 2004	Add Life Medical Institute Ltd. Sterling Hospital Building Ahmedabad	USA	326.24	7.07

Source: Quoted from Chanda (undated)

Nevertheless, the government had to maintain a fine balance between the commitment to reform and social commitments. When the NDA government was defeated in 2004 general election, and the same was considered to be a mandate against hasty reforms, the succeeding UPA government was quick to follow the path of social commitments. The subsequent decisions taken through National Common Minimum Programme (NCMP) to increase public spending on health to at least 2-3 per cent of GDP over the next five years, and stepping up public investment in programmes to control all communicable diseases etc. need to be viewed in this light. However, Rao and Choudhury (2012) note that the effectiveness of the Central Government budgetary devolution under this category has been limited because 'low-income states could not avail the grants by making their own contributions and could not afford to pay for the current component of spending.'

The growing realization of the limitations of the public health schemes and networks to ensure health security domestically as well as medical service exports, has helped the Government of India to increasingly realize importance of involving private players. It was felt that the reforms, though welcomed by the private sector, were not doing enough to ensure that healthcare be made available to the low-income citizens. Therefore, provision of land and other incentives to private players to enhance their reach in return of free / concessional treatment of the poor was considered to be a way out (Qadeer and Reddy, 2006). Advocating the importance of different forms of PPPs in India, the Planning Commission (2004) noted:

> "A closer look at the poor performance of *public utilities and social services,* in general, also shows that the disease lies in the 'monopoly' characteristic of such activities. Since there is no alternative to the existing *(in-house)* service providers, the citizens are left with no option other than that of *"take it or leave it"*. The executives/ bureaucracy (low & high) may thus take the liberty to indulge in lethargy, corruption and high handedness. It has, therefore, been commented that the important distinction is not public versus private *rather it is monopoly versus competition.* In this respect, PPP may be looked at as a measure towards administrative reforms."

In line with the PPP consensus, in 2005 the National Rural Health Mission (NRHM) was introduced, which was given the responsibility of bridging the healthcare gaps and ensuring *decentralized* healthcare. The idea was to ensure affordable healthcare in rural areas, which had historically been understaffed. NRHM (2005-12) was introduced in 18 Indian states for ensuring a network of one ASHA (Accredited Social Health Activist) per 1000 people. The NRHM goals included reduction in Infant Mortality Rate (IMR) and Maternal Mortality Ratio (MMR), universal access to public health services (e.g. women and child health, immunization, nutrition), prevention and control of communicable and non-communicable diseases etc. NRHM focuses on strengthening of existing Primary Health Centres (PHC) and upgrading of 3222 existing Community Health Centers (30-50 beds) to 24-Hour First Referral Units (NRHM Mission Document). The Document acknowledged the role of the PPPs in improving access to healthcare for the population and noted the need for, 'identifying areas of partnership, which are need based, thematic and geographic'. Along similar lines, in 2006 the decision to form a National Urban Health Mission (NUHM) was taken:

> "In terms of urban health care strategies, the Task Force recommends a) an Urban Health Centre (UHCs) catering to every 50,000 population (which is anticipated to include about 25,000 urban poor); b) a Second Tier Health Facility for 250,000 population covering 5 UHCs and forming a 'Health Zone'." (MHFW, 2006).

The necessity of such a mission was argued to be critical in the light of the growing rural to urban migration and the PPP model was considered crucial for its success.

Since then the optimality of PPPs as a sustainable model has been noted widely (Baru and Nundy, 2008). For instance, the initiatives include government partnerships with leading private players like Apollo (Thomas and Krishnan, 2010). Moreover, on several occasions, foreign players have partnered Indian government and domestic private players for delivering healthcare services (Singh, 2011). The decision to allow foreign players to enter the Indian market by paving the way for smoother FDI in the health sector needs to be viewed against this broader canvas.

Nevertheless, there is a need to understand the shift in policy framework in light of the government motivation, i.e. whether the government truly believes in the reform philosophy or is simply trying to pass part of its fiscal burden to the private sector. In case of the former the PPP is likely to secure an efficient outcome. WEF (undated) has noted that, 'PPP is to achieve a mission that calls for skills, capabilities and resources beyond what each organization possesses individually.' Such realization on part of the government is indeed welcome. However, in case of the latter, the partnerships may not be able to fulfill their objectives. In the following, the PPP experience in India is critically assessed through a literature survey.

Public-Private Partnerships in India: How Effective?

The PPP partners of the government are generally selected through a process of competitive bidding and competitive negotiation. Rajsulochana and Dash (2009) observed that PPPs fall under different categories in terms of goals, namely: increasing access (mobile health units), affordability (community health insurance), efficiency (functional autonomy to hospitals), financing (joint ventures), outreach (partnering with grassroots organization), risk transfer (contracting) etc. Gupta (2009) noted that examples of PPPs include 'outsourcing of hospital maintenance, operationalisation and management of state and district data centre, radiology services, pathology services, etc.'. Under the PPPs, user charges for patients have been introduced, though they are much cheaper than would be charged by the private sector. The BPL households are required to pay a nominal fee and specialist physicians are paid a per unit fee as an incentive.

Several successful PPP models have emerged over the last few years. Basu (undated) has noted that Rashtriya Swasthya Bima Yojana (RSBY), which was launched in 2008, has been quite successful in enhancing health coverage for BPL households in India. Here the insurer receives a premium for each enrolled household, while a hospital is 'paid per beneficiary treated'. The private sector contributes to the system by helping in the search of BPL households and getting paid for their services. Shende et al (2009) noted that in Maharashtra a good viable model has been introduced by the collaboration between Municipal Corporation of Greater Mumbai (entrusted with services and infrastructure provision), community (problem identification and monitoring of the project), ICICI Centre for Child Health and Nutrition (funding), Centre for International Health and Development (input design, evaluation and dissemination), SNEHA (implementation and monitoring). A considerable degree of health infrastructure has been created and referral links with hospitals have been established. Bhattacharya and Rahman (2010) notes that the contracting model has worked well in those states where BPL patients receive free testing facilities:

> "In Rajsthan, Orissa and Tamil Nadu, diagnostic services and equipment in Medical College hospitals are built by private sector, in the space provided. Once equipment is in place, doctors are required to refer patients to these centers for treatment - charges decided by the Government".

Despite the success of these and other PPPs, there are those which have failed. There is a need to understand the underlying reasons behind the failures. Raman (2009) notes that PPPs formed after mutual consultation have performed better vis-à-vis competitively selected partners. However, Mukhopadhyay (undated) noted that the NGOs have limited say during the health planning stage. Raman (2009) also observes that as the government lacks the requisite technical and managerial skills to run successful PPPs, the 'visionary' individuals have played crucial roles. The government policy of periodic transfer of officials therefore has often hurt the operation of successful PPPs. The other reasons behind failures include: hasty planning; untimely budgetary devolution from the government; mismatch between grassroots needs and government agenda; government inefficiency and red tape; greater emphasis on achieving the quantitative target, rather than ensuring the quality of the service; political interference; and failure to devise sufficient in-built incentives etc. (Gupta, 2009; Sewa Rural Team, 2004; Elamon, 2004; Kapadia, 2004; Sen, 2004; Raman and Björkman, undated; Mukhopadhyay, undated).

Gupta (2009) indicated the absence of proper due diligence during the PPP planning stages by quoting the following example:

> "Decentralisation of decision making powers to local levels were absent in many cases which led to bizarre situations. In one of the district hospitals, hardly 100 kilometres from the state capital, there were three X-ray units in adjacent rooms; one run by the government staff which didn't charge any fees from patients, another run by a charitable trust at subsidised cost and the third through PPP because the state government had entered with a Memorandum of Understanding (MOU) with the PSP!"

Singh (2011) quotes the example of Jalandhar Hospital and Medical College as another example of PPP failure, where an NRI group was part of the PPP. The responsibility of the private partner was to provide all equipment and staff and also to ensure free treatment to BPL patients. However, after starting operation in mid-2010, the private player backed off from its commitment to free treatment for the BPL population, and subsequently the Medical Council of India revoked its approval to the medical college, disqualifying it from granting medical degrees.

The Future

The dismal performance of several PPP initiatives begs the larger question of whether the government considers PPPs as a 'private initiative supported by the public sector' or a 'public initiative supplemented by the private sector'. This is extremely crucial, because if the former is the underlying motive, then the government role will be reduced in the long term to a mere facilitator, and efficiency will automatically be augmented with increasing operational flexibility of private partners. However in case the latter mindset prevails, the PPP will always be 'controlled' by the government in keeping with the principle of helping the poorest section of the population, despite the potential decrease in the efficiency of the healthcare arrangements. Despite the continuing stream of reforms, the government appears to be maintaining its paternalist and interventionist attitude to the health sector. The mindset is exemplified by a recent statement of the Union Health Minister, Mr. Ghulam Nabi Azad, in the Indian Parliament on the need to regulate drug prices:

> "The Ministry of Health & Family Welfare has prepared the National List of Essential Medicines (NLEM), 2011 consisting of 348 medicines. This Ministry has requested the DoP, which administers the Drug Price Control Order (DPCO) to bring all drugs in the NLEM, 2011 under the price control," (Shankar, 2012).

However, such a step, once implemented, will go against the spirit of the ongoing reforms. The number of drugs on the DPCO list was around 347 in the 1970s, declining to around 300 in the early 1980s, and subsequently falling to 140 in 1987. Presently, 74 bulk drugs and formulations are supposed to follow the price control regime (Sengupta et al, undated). Expansion of the list would reduce company profitability (and consequently to a decline in research and development expenditure) without substantial improvement in consumer welfare. Along similar lines, in the healthcare sector, often the required thrust towards reforms is missing.

Therefore, adoption of a liberal healthcare policy regime will help India in both the domestic and international front on several counts. First, the time is ripe to let efficient private players in the healthcare sector grow and enhance their efficiency levels. Only hospitals above a certain standard of operation can hope for accreditation by Joint Commission International (JCI) / Joint Commission for the Accreditation of Hospitals and Healthcare Organizations (JCAHO). These standards are based on all the health related parameters including quality of patient care, accessibility, personal and equipment hygiene, etc. Apollo hospitals group has been the first Indian entity to receive JCI accreditation (Clark University, 2010), and several other Indian hospitals have received the same since then. Allowing a greater role for large reputable private players can expand the list further. Collaboration with foreign entities, through FDI and other forms of collaborations, would have a crucial role in this regard.

Second, increased rates of medical tourism and lack of portability of medical insurance for foreign patients have forced the private players either to enter into tie-ups with foreign insurance players or actively advertise in various media in India and abroad. The deepening of the health insurance schemes offered jointly by Indian and foreign players (e.g. Birla Sun Life health insurance, ICICI Prudential health insurance) is another example of market based solutions on this front (HT, 2009). Also a number of tour operators have come forward to take advantage of this development (e.g. Kuoni - Apollo, Cox & Kings - Dr. Batras, Vedic India etc.) and easing foreign participation in this segment will also be quite relevant. Greater reforms in the insurance sector in general and in the area of health reform in particular is the need of the hour.

Third, the PPPs have contributed considerably so far in the creation of health infrastructure in India. But as indicated earlier, their ability for better delivery is often constrained by the improper handling from the government partner. Greater understanding from the government is greatly needed to secure the best output from existing collaborations. Crucially, the government must grant greater autonomy to the private partners at all stages (planning, execution as well as assessment). Only then can an optimal outcome from the PPP initiatives be expected.

Note

1. Assistant Professor of Economics, Indian Institute of Foreign Trade, New Delhi. The views expressed by the author are his own.

Bibliography

Bangdiwala, Shrikant I., Joseph D. Tucker, Sanjay Zodpey, Sian M. Grifiths, Li-Ming Li, K. Srinath Reddy, Myron S. Cohen, Miriam Gross, Kavya Sharma, Jin-Ling Tang (2011), 'Public Health Education in India and China: History, Opportunities, and Challenges', *Public Health Reviews*, 33(1): 204-224.

Baru, Rama (undated), 'Privatisation of Health Care in India: A Comparative Analysis of Orissa, Karnataka and Maharashtra States', As part of the Project "Economic Reforms, and Health Sector in India", under the aegis of United Nations Development Programme (UNDP)and Government of India, New Delhi.

Baru, Rama and Madhurima Nundy (2008), 'Blurring of Boundaries: Public-Private partnerships in Health Services in India', *Economic and Political Weekly*, 43(4): 62-71.

Basu, Rumki (undated), 'Rashtriya Swasthya Bima Yojana: Pioneering Public-Private Partnership in Health Insurance', available at http://www.napsipag.org/PDF/RUMKI%20BASU.pdf(last accessed on November10, 2012).

Bhattacharya, Debapriya and Mustafizur Rahman (2010), 'Delivering Social Infrastructure through PPP: The Role of Non-Profit Organisation', presented at the OECD Global Forum on Development, Paris, 10-12 October.

Chakraborty, Debashis and Anuj Dilwaria (2011), 'India's Growing Presence in Health Services Trade? Challenges and Policy Options', *Taiwanese Journal of WTO Studies*, 20: 1-45.

Chakraborty, Debashis and Pavel Chakraborty (2009), 'The Health Scenario in India: A Cross-State Analysis', in P. Stevens and D. Chakraborty (Eds.), "Towards a Healthy Future? Indian and Global Experiences", pp. 89-130, Bookwell, New Delhi.

Chanda, Rupa (2001), 'Trade In Health Services', ICRIER Working Paper No. 70, New Delhi.

Chanda, Rupa (undated), 'Foreign Investment in Hospitals in India: Status and Implications', Project In collaboration with WHO India Country Office, New Delhi and WTO Cell, Ministry of Health and Family Welfare, Government of India.

Clark University (2010), 'Investing In India: A Guide to U.S. Investors', Graduate School of Management, Worcester, MA.

Dhar, Aarti (2012), 'The expanding cover', The Hindu, October 18, Chennai.

Elamon, Joy (2004), 'Health Sector Reforms: Initiatives in Kerala and the Lessons', presented in the National Seminar on "Health Sector Reforms: A Cross-State Comparison of Public-Private Partnership and Community Initiatives", jointly organized by Indian Council of Social Science Research and Centre de Sciences Humaines, 30 -31 August.

Government of India (1983), 'National Health Policy', Ministry of Health and Family Welfare, New Delhi.

Government of India (2002), 'National Health Policy', Ministry of Health and Family Welfare, New Delhi.

Government of India (2004), 'Report of the Public Private Partnership Sub-Group on Social Sector', Planning Commission, New Delhi.

Government of India(2004), 'National Common Minimum Programme', Prime Minister's Office, New Delhi.

Government of India (2005), 'National Rural Health Mission (2005-2012): Mission Document' Ministry of Health, New Delhi.

Government of India (2006), 'Draft Final Report of the Task Force to Advise the National Rural Health Mission on "Strategies for Urban Health Care"', Ministry of Health & Family Welfare, New Delhi.

Government of India (2012), 'Economic Survey 2011-12', Ministry of Finance, New Delhi.

Gupta, Indrani, Bishwanath Goldar and Arup Mitra (1998), 'The Case of India', UNCTAD-WHO Joint Publication, *International Trade in Health Services: A Development Perspective*, Chapter 13, Geneva.

Gupta, Mona (2011), 'Public Private Partnership (PPP) Initiatives in Bihar: Successes and Failures', presented in the Conference on "Emerging health care models: Engaging the private health sector", YMCA, Mumbai, 25th - 26th September.

High Commission of India, Colombo (2011), 'India—Connects', The Economic and Business Newsletter, Vol II(2), available at http://www.hcicolombo.org/pdf/India_Connect.pdf (last accessed on October 8, 2012).

Hindustan Times (2009), 'Health is Hot: 4 new Firms Soon', September 7, New Delhi.

Indian Express (2011), 'MCI gives nod to 21 new colleges, adds 1,800 seats', July 1, Mumbai.

Kapadia, L.A. (2004), 'Issues concerning the Rogi Kalyan Samiti in Madhya Pradesh', presented in the National Seminar on "Health Sector Reforms: A Cross-State Comparison of Public-Private Partnership and Community Initiatives", jointly organized by Indian Council of Social Science Research and Centre de Sciences Humaines, 30-31 August.

Medical Council of India (undated), 'Annual Reports' (various issues) available at http://www.mciindia.org/AboutMCI/Annual Reports .aspx (last accessed on 19 October, 2012).

Mukhopadhyay, Alok (undated), 'Public-Private Partnership inthe Health Sector in India', available at http://www.uhrc.in/uhgateway/documents/1073.pdf(last accessed on October26, 2012).

Narayan, Jayaprakash (2009), 'Ensuring a Healthy Future', in P. Stevens and D. Chakraborty (Eds.), "Towards a Healthy Future? Indian and Global Experiences", pp. 231-92, Bookwell, New Delhi.

Pandav, Chandrakant S. (2007), 'Health Sector Reform in India', presented at the International Workshop on "Public-Private Mix: a Public Health Fix? Strategies for Health Sector Reform in South and Southeast Asia", Naresuan University, Phitsanulok, Thailand, 20-22 June.

Qadeer, Imrana and Sunita Reddy (2006), 'Medical Care in the Shadow of Public Private Partnership', *Social Scientist*, 34(9-10): 4-20.

Rajsulochana and Umakant Dash (2009), 'The Economics behind Public Private Partnerships (PPP) in Health Sector', presented in the Conference on "Emerging health care models: Engaging the private health sector", YMCA, Mumbai, 25th – 26th September.

Raman, A Venkat and James Warner Björkman (undated), 'Public/Private Partnership in Health Care Services in India', available at http://www.pppinharyana.gov.in/ppp/sector/health/report-healthcare.pdf(last accessed on November8, 2012).

Raman, A. Venkat (undated), 'Public/Private Partnership in Health Care Service delivery in India', available at http://urban-india.com/pdf/Raman_ Public%20private%20partnership%20in% 20health%20service%20delivery%20in%20India.pdf(last accessed on November4, 2012).

Raman, A. Venkat (2009), 'Public Private Partnerships in health services' presented in the Conference on "Emerging health care models: Engaging the private health sector", YMCA, Mumbai, 25th – 26th September.

Rao, M. Govinda and Mita Choudhury (2012), 'Health Care Financing Reforms in India', National Institute of Public Finance and Policy Working Paper, New Delhi.

Sen, Binayak (2004), 'The Myth of the Mitanin: Political Constraints on Structural Reforms in Health Care in Chhattisgarh', presented in the National Seminar on "Health Sector Reforms: A Cross-State Comparison of Public-Private Partnership and Community Initiatives", jointly organized by Indian Council of Social Science Research and Centre de Sciences Humaines, 30-31 August.

Sengupta, Amit, Reji K. Joseph,Shilpa Modi and Nirmalya Syam (undated), 'Economic Constraints to Access to Essential Medicines in India', Society for Economic and Social Studies and Centre for Trade and Development in collaboration with WHO India Country Office, New Delhi.

Sewa Rural Team (2004), 'Making of a Primary Health Centre: The SEWA Rural's Experiment of NGO-GO Partnership', presented in the National Seminar on "Health Sector Reforms: A Cross-State Comparison of Public-Private Partnership and Community Initiatives", jointly organized by Indian Council of Social Science Research and Centre de Sciences Humaines, 30-31 August.

Shankar, Ramesh *(2012)*, 'NPPA issues internal guidelines for price fixation/revision of bulk drugs under DPCO, 1995', November 9, available at http://pharmabiz.com/NewsDetails.aspx?aid=72079&sid=1(last accessed on November 6, 2012).

Shende, Sushma, Jaya Nuty, Surekha Jagtap, Sapna Gaikwad, Trupti Kelkar , Garima Deveshwar- Bahl, David Osrin, Wasundhara Joshi and Armida Fernandez (2009), 'Public Private Partnerships formed by SNEHA: City Initiative For Newborn Health, ASK partnership, Arogya Sarita', presented in the Conference on "Emerging health care models: Engaging the private health sector", YMCA, Mumbai, 25th – 26th September.

Singh, Nirvikar (2011), 'Public-Private Partnerships for Health Care in Punjab', Center for the Advanced Study of India, Working Paper No. 2, University of Pennsylvania, Philadelphia.

Stokes, Bruce (2007), 'Bedside India', *National Journal*, May.

Tendulkar, Suresh D. and T. A. Bhavani (2007), 'Understanding Reforms: Post 1991 India', Oxford University Press, New Delhi.

Thomas, George and Suneeta Krishnan (2010), 'Effective public-private partnership in healthcare: Apollo as a cautionary tale', *Indian Journal of Medical Ethics*, 7(1): 2-4.

World Bank, 'World Development Indicators', available at http://data.worldbank.org/data-catalog/world-development-indicators

World Economic Forum (undated), 'Public-Private Partnerships in Health: The Private Sector's Role in Public-Private Partnerships', available at https://members.weforum.org/pdf/GHI/Partnerships_health.pdf (last accessed on November12, 2012).